BACK

Duke

The Story of Duke's 1992 NCAA Basketball Championship

TO BACK

CHUCK LIDDY • Copyright Durham Herald Co., Inc., 1992

Dedication

This book is dedicated to the memory of Howard "Max" Crowder. For 30 years and 899 straight games, Max was the one constant in Duke basketball. He sat on the Duke bench, with his infamous wide grin, as the team's trainer and best friend at every Duke game since 1962. On December 12, 1991 he was diagnosed with lung cancer and missed his first game, against Michigan, two days later. Max never returned to the Duke bench but a day never went by that he wasn't thought of or talked about. A month after being inducted into the Duke Sports Hall of Fame, Max passed away at the Duke Medical Center on May 28, 1992. Everyone lost a great friend.

FOREWORD

Most fans remember the 1991-92 Duke basketball season as a highlight film: Christian Laettner hits consecutive three-pointers against LSU; Grant Hill swoops under the basket for a reverse dunk in the ACC Tournament finals; Bobby Hurley makes four three-pointers in the first half against Indiana. What we remember, of course, are the thrilling moments, the moments of exhilaration and of victory. Our experience of the 1992 NCAA championship relies on what we have seen, but the success of this team rests more on what we don't see. This book captures well the heat of competition and the excitement of victory. What I want to evoke in this foreword is the invisible foundation on which those moments rest.

As I write, I am looking at a practice schedule from the end of October. Practice has been going on for almost two weeks; there are no games on the immediate horizon. The schedule for this day details two hours of drills - no scrimmage, no chance to play - two hours of work.

What this practice schedule reveals, beneath its laconic, matter-of-fact abbreviations, is the heart of Duke Basketball, the inner force that drives the machine in those glamorous, relatively infrequent games.

Think of the season this way: we saw 36 games; the players and coaches practiced from October 15th until the first week of April. For every game, more than two practices; for every 40 minutes of excitement, more than four hours of drills, conditioning, sheer hard work.

But the schedule reveals more than the mere volume of work. It reveals the careful orchestration of all that effort. Every drill, every simulated game situation, is part of a careful plan. While there is great *expenditure* of effort in every practice, there is also great *efficiency* of effort. None of it is squandered. And so what we see on the court is the finished jewel at the end of a long process. We do not see the mining, the cutting, the polishing - all the processes of refinement without which the beauty of the diamond would remain unrealized.

So, as you read this book, enjoy it. Revel again in the moments it recalls and captures. But also remember and appreciate what underlies those moments: a great, continuing effort by a group of exceptional young men, directed by a coach whose greatest gift lies in *preparing* his players to succeed.

Tom Butters
*Duke University Vice President
Director of Athletics*

```
                              DUKE BASKETBALL
Date    23 Oct                                     Practice No.  8
                          Daily Practice Schedule
TIME:               ACTIVITY:
  3:45-4:00         Pre-Practice   Ind. Work
                      - Contesting Slides (H/R Inside Also)
                      - 5 on 0  Phoenix    -explain Footwork on Top
                      -Bigs - 2 on 0  in the Post
  4:00-4:15         STRETCH
  4:15-4:20         4 Corners - 3 Man Passing Up to F.B.
  4:20-4:25         Zig-Zag, Influence
  4:25-4:30         3 on 3 F.C.
  4:30-4:35         3 Baskets  -  Driving Line
  4:35-4:45         Bigs - Post D
                    Gds - 2 on 2  w/ wing & Post
  4:45-4:55         2 Baskets - 3 on 3 Defense
                       - Contest & Interchange ,  on the same side
  4:55-5:05         Random Movement - Change
                              #41 & #44
  5:05-5:10         Break - Free Throws
  5:10-5:15         Bigs - Shooting to 2 on 0
                    Per.  -  2 on 0 Shooting
  5:15-5:25         Bigs - 2 on 2 P/E
                    Per. - 2 on 2 add Post
  5:25-5:35         2 Baskets - 2 on 2 Post & Per Screening
                              (Change spots)
v&s 5:35-5:45       Motion -  5 on 5
                         Slide & Talk
     Notes:   1. Check on Training Meal
              2. LIFT
              3. Scrimmage 3:45 Wed.
              4. #2 & #3 Hold & Cross Tomorrow before the scrimmage
                 #4 Low
```

Mike Krzyzewski's practice plan for October 23, 1991

contents

CHUCK LIDDY

"Back To Back - *The Story of Duke's 1992 NCAA Basketball Championship* **"**
was produced by Mike Cragg, Director of Sports Information, Duke University

Layout and Design: John Roth; Moore Marketing, Inc.; Durham, NC
Cover Design: Jim Jarvis; West Side Studio; Durham, NC
Printing: Delmar Printing & Publishing; Charlotte, NC
Cover Photography: Doug Van de Zande; Van de Zande Photography; Raleigh, NC
Published by: Duke University Press; Durham, NC

A special thanks to sportswriter Bill Brill and all of the photographers who participated in this project.
A special thanks to Chuck Liddy of the Durham Herald-Sun and Tony Glasson from Delmar Printing & Publishing
for their dedication to the book.

1 BACK **Duke** TO BACK

The Story
of Duke's
1992
NCAA
Basketball
Championship

Meeting Every Challenge

By Mike Krzyzewski

CHUCK LIDDY

THIS 1991-92 DUKE BASKETBALL TEAM DID A SENSA-
tional job. It was my most rewarding and best year in
coaching. When you consider everything we
accomplished and the fact that we were number
one all year long, it was truly incredible. We really got
everybody's best shot and in being number one, our
guys never let down.

Our road to the Final Four and ultimately to win

the national championship was the toughest road we ever had to face. We had to play a very difficult Seton Hall team, a tremendous Kentucky team, Indiana in the semifinals, and an extremely talented group of young men in Michigan to win the national championship. It also came at a time of the year where I didn't know if our team could get emotional enough. The last two games the wear and tear began to show and we had to wait a half to get emotional enough. But what I love is that there was a lot of emotion left in my team and they rose to the occasion.

I don't think it has sunk in yet as far as the two years in a row because we as a group tried to look at this 1992 season as only this

season. We never looked at "defending" a national championship but rather the pursuit of another title. We tried to look at it as having fun and I think we played the toughest schedule in the country. We tried to achieve and have fun along the way. It wasn't until we beat a great Kentucky team in an incredible basketball game where we could start talking about an opportunity to win the national championship.

Something that made this championship maybe more difficult was the way we went through the NCAA Tournament. Last year when we won the Midwest Regional we beat St. John's and when we got back no one talked about the St. John's game because we won big and everyone knew we had to play UNLV. That made it easier to focus on Vegas, our next opponent.

This season, winning the way we did against Kentucky, everybody wanted to talk about Kentucky. When you have an emotional experience like that it's only natural to want to live it over and over again. So for these guys to stay focused so well and win against Indiana and then to still have enough to beat Michigan, is one of the more incredible things a team has done for me in my 17 years of coaching.

When I looked at our team against Michigan in the first half, I was wondering what might happen. We weren't really functioning completely as a unit. In the end, however, it was another example of our entire team coming together. We got key contributions, not just against Michigan but against Indiana, from our bench which we definitely needed to win. All season long when adversity would strike, like injuries, our team would come together.

I thought in the week of practice before the Final Four our blue team (reserves) practiced the best they had all season long. They simulated tough competition for the regulars

to get ready. It not only helped the starters but it helped the whole team at the Final Four.

Cherokee Parks helped us a lot in both games and Marty Clark making those free throws against Indiana was exciting to see. Everyone picked it up when we needed it most.

Grant Hill was phenomenal against Michigan but that wasn't surprising because he played that way all year long. His ability to play virtually anywhere on the court gave us a dimension that few teams can duplicate.

When Brian Davis got hurt badly against Indiana, I really felt there was no way he could play at all against Michigan. He spent the 48 hours after that game doing all kinds of therapy with our trainers. In the end, Brian was there when we needed him. The thing I'll remember, was in the second half, when he probably shouldn't have played, he was able to come in for a short time and give Thomas and Grant a break.

Brian was the best leader for our team and he became an excellent overall player. Believe me, he helps us in more ways than anyone will ever know except me.

One of the great stories of the whole season was after we had our injuries someone needed to step up. Over the last two months of the season, Tony Lang was that man. He did whatever it took and ended up starting every game after Grant's injury. The thing I liked about Tony, and really all of our guys, was how much improvement he showed over the course of the year. That is the sign of a great team and Tony made us a great team.

Probably the guy who is overlooked a lot is Thomas Hill. The most excited I got in the title game was in the second half when Thomas takes a shot from about 12 feet and misses and Grant somehow gets a hand on it and keeps it alive. Then I don't know how Thomas gets the ball but he does and he puts it in. It's that kind of competitiveness which sets him apart. I'm sure other teams have competitive

kids, but Thomas goes further than anyone I know.

All year long the two guys that were our key guys as far as setting the tempo for the team were the little guy up on top and the big guy inside. Bobby Hurley was named MVP of the Final Four and it's impossible to single out any one play but the confident expression he had made me more confident and I know it made his teammates more confident. It was the same look he had last year when we won the national championship.

Christian Laettner will always be remembered, not only for what he accomplished but his jersey will be hanging in Cameron Indoor Stadium. Everyone knows about all the records he broke but to me, at this Final Four, at the end of a very exhausting year he was still terrific. Against Indiana his rebounding in the second half and his defensive play was sensational. And against Michigan, I think what Christian did in the second half, after

BOB DONNAN

the way he played in the first half, made me appreciate him even more. I'm not sure if any players, at any level, would have done what he did in the second half.

I also want to thank our sixth man for being an integral part of our team this year. I thought late in February when I made some comments about us sitting on our hands instead of clapping, that it was taken the right way. One of the things I try to instill in our team is to always be hungry - not to take

anything for granted, to appreciate the moment and not just expect the next moment. You have to work for the next moment so that when it happens it means something. This championship means something because we've all invested in it.

I loved my team last year, but this team was a great team. It met every challenge and at the Final Four it showed its true personality by winning both games in the second half with what I like best, defense.

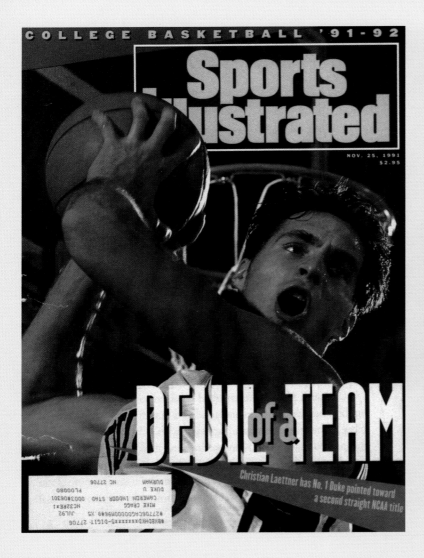

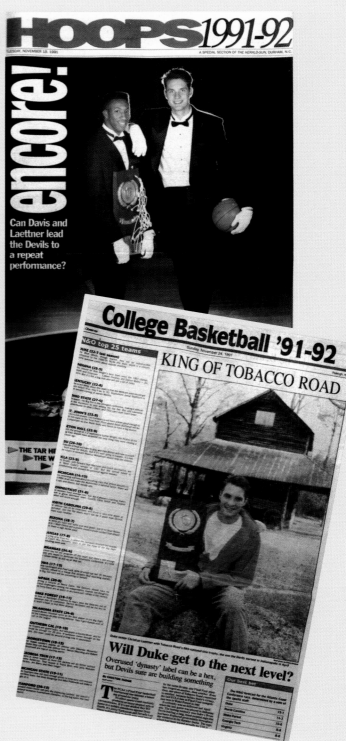

With America's number one ranked team and the projected player of the year, Duke was college basketball's most popular preseason cover story – locally and nationally – during the autumn of 1991.

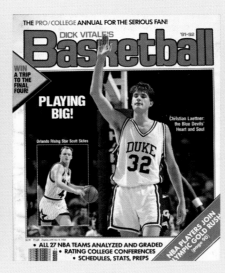

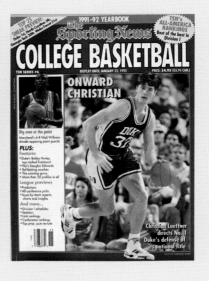

A national television audience looked on for the exhibition game between basketball's super powers, Duke University and the Soviets. It marked the debut of a rising power in freshman **Cherokee Parks** as he thrilled the crowd with 19 points and four blocked shots in the 90-70 victory. On four occasions, Parks followed his own score by blocking a shot at the other end of the court. A reverse dunk by Parks and **Grant Hill's** Jordanesque slam after taking off from the foul line were crowd favorites. **Thomas Hill** and **Antonio Lang** watched the game from the bench with minor injuries as Duke took a 30-21 halftime lead and put together a 14-2 run in the second half to take command. **Erik Meek** played 15 minutes in his collegiate debut.

> Cherokee's in that same ballpark where Christian Laettner was as a freshman or Danny Ferry was. Cherokee's every bit as good at that point in his career. Hopefully, he will become as good as his career continues.
> *– Mike Krzyzewski*

CHUCK LIDDY

November 23, 1991
Cameron Indoor Stadium, Durham, NC

Soviet Union	Min	FG M-A	FT M-A	Reb O-T	A	TP
Antipov	31	3-7	2-2	1-4	2	8
Grachev	33	3-7	4-4	5-7	2	11
Kondatov	19	4-10	2-2	1-3	0	11
Mikhailov	21	3-7	0-0	4-7	2	6
Grezin	35	8-17	4-4	1-6	1	21
Olbreht	20	4-9	0-0	2-6	0	8
Fetisov	18	0-1	0-1	0-6	0	0
Chernov	19	1-3	1-2	1-2	2	3
Kudelin	3	1-1	0-0	0-0	0	2
Kurashov	1	0-0	0-0	0-0	0	0
Totals	200	27-72	13-15	18-46	9	70

Duke	Min	FG M-A	FT M-A	Reb O-T	A	TP
Hurley	36	8-14	4-5	0-3	7	22
G. Hill	31	8-9	6-7	1-5	3	22
Laettner	25	5-15	1-1	1-3	1	12
Davis	33	4-8	0-1	1-5	1	8
Parks	22	8-11	3-4	3-8	0	19
Clark	14	0-4	2-2	1-1	2	2
Blakeney	17	2-4	1-3	1-1	1	5
Meek	15	0-1	0-4	0-2	1	0
Ast	4	0-2	0-0	1-4	0	0
Burt	3	0-0	0-0	0-0	0	0
Totals	200	35-68	17-27	11-37	16	90

Soviet Union	39	31	70
Duke	51	39	90

FG Pct: Soviet Union 37.5, Duke 51.5
FT Pct: Soviet Union 86.7, Duke 63.0
3FG Shooting: Soviet Union 3-10 (Grezin 1-2, Grachev 1-3, Kondatov 1-3, Olbreht 0-1, Chernov 0-1); Duke 3-6 (Hurley 2-3, Laettner 1-3).
Turnovers: Soviet Union 26, Duke 18
Blocks: Soviet Union 4, Duke 8 (Parks 4)
Steals: Soviet Union 8, Duke 6 (Hurley 2)
Fouled Out: Mikhailov, Grezin
Officials: Hightower, Moreau, Ferguson
Attendance: 9,314

Christian Laettner missed the only game of his collegiate career in the 1991-92 season opener against East Carolina. Laettner suffered a bruised foot against the Soviet Selects to break a streak of 86 straight starts going into the game. Duke handled the loss well in scoring a 103-75 victory over the Pirates.

Cherokee Parks made all five of his field goal attempts in his first collegiate start, including this hook over Anton Gill. Parks also grabbed eight rebounds and blocked four shots to spark the Blue Devils.

Leading all scorers in the season opener was **Bobby Hurley** who had 20 points. He also dished out seven assists in playing 29 minutes for Duke.

"

This has a tremendous effect on my confidence. I come off the bench and contribute as much as I can. Eventually, I'll develop to the level where I can help the team in the big games.
– *Marty Clark*
Career-high 17 points

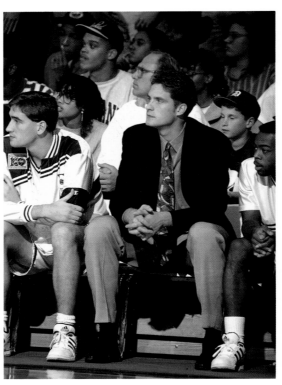

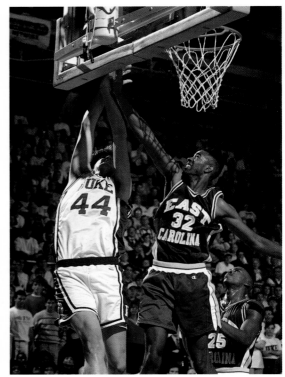

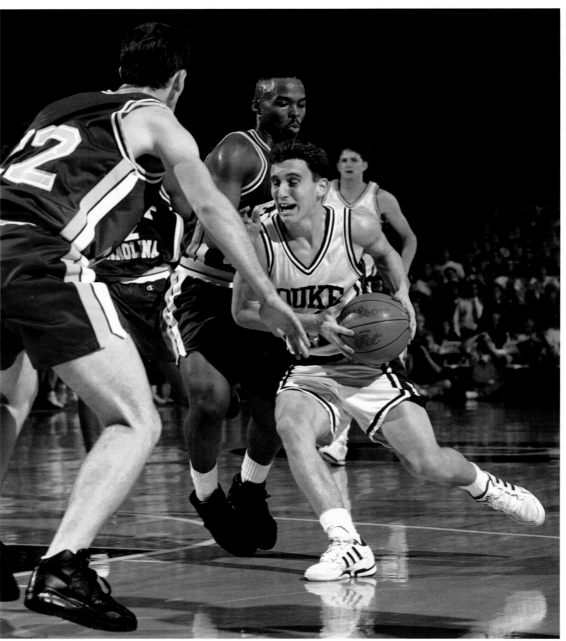

November 25, 1991
Cameron Indoor Stadium, Durham, NC

East Carolina	Min	FG M-A	FT M-A	Reb O-T	A	TP
Lyons	32	9-19	5-5	1-4	3	27
House	5	0-1	0-0	0-0	0	0
Peterson	26	2-6	2-4	1-3	4	6
Gill	25	4-4	1-2	3-3	0	9
Copeland	31	4-10	1-6	2-7	1	9
Young	27	7-13	2-2	3-3	2	16
Childress	19	0-3	0-0	0-1	2	0
Armstrong	16	2-4	0-0	1-2	0	4
Lewis	10	2-2	0-0	0-0	0	4
Richardson	6	0-2	0-0	0-0	1	0
Perlich	3	0-0	0-0	0-0	0	0
Totals	200	30-64	11-19	11-25	13	75

Duke	Min	FG M-A	FT M-A	Reb O-T	A	TP
Hurley	29	6-8	7-9	0-0	7	20
T. Hill	24	6-11	3-3	0-1	0	16
Davis	32	1-4	3-4	0-6	2	5
G. Hill	27	6-14	3-4	1-6	3	15
Parks	20	5-5	6-8	2-8	1	16
Clark	22	6-8	3-3	3-5	4	17
Meek	17	4-5	1-5	2-6	0	9
Blakeney	17	0-0	0-0	0-0	4	0
Burt	5	0-0	2-2	0-0	1	2
Ast	7	1-3	1-1	0-1	0	3
Totals	200	35-58	29-39	11-37	22	103

East Carolina	29	46	75
Duke	46	57	103

FG Pct: East Carolina 46.9, Duke 60.3
FT Pct: East Carolina 57.9, Duke 74.4
3FG Shooting: ECU 4-12 (Lyons 4-9, Peterson 0-1, Young 0-1, Richardson 0-1); Duke 4-8 (Clark 2-2, Hurley 1-2, T. Hill 1-2, Ast 0-2)
Turnovers: East Carolina 23, Duke 20
Blocks: East Carolina 2, Duke 5 (Parks 3)
Steals: East Carolina 8, Duke 9 (T. Hill, Clark 3)
Fouled Out: House, Childress
Officials: Rose, Gordon, Allen
Attendance: 9,314

Duke crushed the visiting Harvard Crimson 118-65 in the largest margin of victory all season. Eight Blue Devils scored in double-figures, including **Brian Davis.** Duke shot an impressive 68 percent from the field while **Erik Meek** and **Christian Ast** got significant playing time. The 118 points marked the eighth highest point total in school history. **Christian Laettner** returned to the starting lineup with 10 points in 15 minutes of action.

"

We know we're playing big games in the future. This is preparation for those big games. You can't play sloppy one night and excellent the next night.
– *Thomas Hill*

BOB DONNAN

November 30, 1991
Cameron Indoor Stadium, Durham, NC

Harvard	Min	FG M-A	FT M-A	Reb O-T	A	TP
Leake	29	6-12	1-2	0-0	5	14
McLain	28	6-10	0-0	2-3	4	15
Minor	25	2-5	0-0	2-4	1	4
Rullman	30	4-8	0-0	2-4	0	8
Mitchell	18	3-5	1-2	0-4	2	7
Condakes	16	4-12	0-0	1-3	0	8
White	15	3-5	0-0	0-0	0	7
Jabbar-Abdi	13	0-1	0-0	0-2	0	0
Carter	9	0-1	0-2	0-2	1	0
Chhabra	11	1-4	0-0	1-4	0	2
LaPointe	3	0-0	0-0	0-0	2	0
Scott	2	0-1	0-1	0-1	0	0
Kubiak	1	0-1	0-1	1-1	0	0
Totals	200	29-65	2-8	12-32	15	65

Duke	Min	FG M-A	FT M-A	Reb O-T	A	TP
Hurley	23	4-8	3-5	0-1	4	13
T. Hill	18	8-10	0-2	1-1	4	17
Laettner	15	3-4	4-4	0-2	3	10
G. Hill	25	7-8	3-5	1-3	5	17
Davis	22	3-6	4-4	0-3	3	10
Parks	22	6-6	3-5	0-6	0	15
Clark	20	3-8	2-4	2-4	1	10
Blakeney	18	5-5	2-3	1-4	2	12
Meek	16	1-3	4-7	0-3	1	6
Ast	13	1-2	2-2	2-5	1	4
Burt	8	2-3	0-0	0-0	4	4
Totals	200	43-63	27-41	9-34	28	118

Harvard	28	37	65
Duke	59	59	118

FG Pct: Harvard 44.6, Duke 68.3
FT Pct: Harvard 25.0, Duke 65.9
3FG Shooting: Harvard 5-11 (McLain 3-4, Leake 1-2, White 1-2, Minor 0-1, Rullman 0-1, Condares 0-1); Duke 5-10 (Clark 2-3, Hurley 2-5, T. Hill 1-2)
Turnovers: Harvard 26, Duke 12
Blocks: Harvard 1, Duke 8 (Parks 4)
Steals: Harvard 4, Duke 11 (T. Hill 3)
Fouled Out: McLain, Mitchell, White
Officials: Gray, Hess, Elliott
Attendance: 9,314

Duke's players left no doubt in the first 30 minutes of their game against seventh-ranked St. John's that they deserved the nation's top ranking again in 1992. A clinic was the only way to describe Duke's domination of the Redmen as the Blue Devils opened a whopping 31-point lead on the way to a 91-81 victory in the final segment of the ACC/Big East Challenge in Greensboro. **Christian Laettner** had 26 points and converted 13-of-13 free throws to run his school record free throw streak to 31. (He eventually finished with 35 made in a row.) Duke went on a 12-0 streak at the beginning of the game high-lighted by a **Grant Hill** dunk. St. John's coach Lou Carnesecca called timeout at the 16:49 mark but could not stop the ongoing rout. Duke widened the margin to 28-12 and eventually 48-30 at halftime with its patented pressure defense. After St. John's scored the first four points of the second half, Duke gave the entire nation something to talk about over morning coffee the next day. The Blue Devils put on a 20-3 run in the next five minutes, exclamated by a **Bobby Hurley** to Grant Hill alley-oop dunk perfected eight months earlier in Indianapolis. The Duke defense was all over the court in forcing 21 turnovers and leading to numerous fast break opportunities. St. John's senior Malik Sealy prevented a total embarrassment for his team by scoring 37 points and cutting Duke's winning margin to a respectable amount. Duke was now 3-0 and had the attention of the entire country but injuries were beginning to mount. Most notable was the tender ankle of **Cherokee Parks**, who suffered a high ankle sprain late in the game. He would miss the next two games entirely and not come back to full strength until midseason.

Holy mackerel, they cut you up so quickly. They dominated every part of the game. Duke made us look bad. Every time they had the ball, they scored. I was told they're 10 to 15 points better than last year, and I have to agree.
– Lou Carnesecca
St. John's coach

KEVIN KEISTER

KEVIN KEISTER

December 5, 1991
Greensboro Coliseum, Greensboro, NC
ACC/Big East Challenge

Duke	Min	FG M-A	FT M-A	Reb O-T	A	TP
Davis	28	3-5	1-1	1-3	2	7
G. Hill	24	7-8	1-1	1-3	1	15
Laettner	32	6-12	13-13	1-7	1	26
Hurley	37	2-5	10-12	0-2	8	14
T. Hill	32	3-8	8-8	1-2	2	14
Parks	9	3-6	3-3	1-2	0	9
Clark	12	0-1	1-2	0-0	1	1
Lang	16	0-0	0-2	0-1	0	0
Meek	6	2-2	0-0	0-0	0	4
Blakeney	2	0-0	1-2	0-0	0	1
Ast	1	0-0	0-0	0-0	0	0
Burt	1	0-0	0-0	0-0	0	0
Totals	200	26-47	38-44	7-24	15	91

St. John's	Min	FG M-A	FT M-A	Reb O-T	A	TP
Sealy	36	13-22	9-11	1-6	1	37
Middleton	26	1-3	1-2	2-4	0	3
Werdann	29	2-6	2-2	2-4	0	6
Buchanan	25	1-5	5-8	0-1	3	7
Sproling	24	2-5	0-0	0-1	0	5
Scott	15	2-3	2-2	1-4	0	6
Cain	16	3-7	1-1	1-1	2	7
Green	7	1-1	0-0	0-0	0	2
Foster	13	3-5	0-0	2-3	0	6
Brown	4	1-1	0-0	0-0	0	2
Mullin	5	0-0	0-0	0-0	0	0
Totals	200	29-58	20-26	12-28	6	81

Duke	48	43	91
St. John's	30	51	81

FG Pct: Duke 55.3, St. John's 50.0
FT Pct: Duke 86.4, St. John's 76.9
3FG Shooting: Duke 1-6 (Laettner 1-3, Davis 0-1, Hurley 0-1, T. Hill 0-1); St. John's 3-5 (Sealy 2-2, Sproling 1-1, Buchanan 0-2)
Turnovers: Duke 13, St. John's 21
Blocks: Duke 4 (Laettner 2), St. John's 5
Steals: Duke 6 (G. Hill 4), St. John's 4
Fouled Out: G. Hill, Werdann, Cain
Officials: Wirtz, Donato, Chrisman
Attendance: 15,781

17

Erie County Executive Dennis Gorski declares December 6-8, "Christian Laettner Homecoming Weekend" as the Blue Devils came to town to face Canisius College. Laettner, a product of Angola, NY, played high school basketball at The Nichols School in Buffalo. Members of the Laettner family, including his mother Bonnie and his father George, gathered at the airport to welcome Christian and the rest of the team.

Thomas Hill, however, stole the show at the sold out Buffalo Auditorium, connecting on 9-of-10 field goals for a career-high 26 points. The "other" Hill, **Grant**, added 16 points and 10 rebounds and just missed a "triple-double" with nine assists. **Christian Laettner** passed unselfishly to his teammates as he had six assists in leading Duke to a 32-12 lead in the game's first 13 minutes and a 47-25 halftime margin. Christian's night turned out to be the largest crowd to ever witness a college basketball game in the Aud as 16,279 gathered to welcome him home.

"

I expected it to be an exciting situation for me and my teammates. It was all that I expected. To see the Aud sold out...I can remember coming here as a kid and watching games and the place wasn't even half filled.
– *Christian Laettner*

December 7, 1991
Buffalo Auditorium, Buffalo, NY

Duke	Min	FG M-A	FT M-A	Reb O-T	A	TP
Hurley	18	2-5	2-2	0-2	4	7
T. Hill	29	9-10	6-6	1-3	1	26
Davis	26	2-7	4-4	2-6	0	8
Laettner	35	6-10	7-8	2-5	6	19
G. Hill	34	6-7	4-8	1-10	9	16
Clark	15	3-3	0-0	0-1	1	7
Blakeney	5	1-1	2-2	0-2	0	4
Burt	2	1-1	0-0	0-0	0	2
Lang	21	0-2	1-2	1-5	0	1
Meek	12	2-2	0-2	0-2	0	4
Ast	3	0-0	2-2	0-0	0	2
Totals	200	32-48	28-36	7-37	21	96

Canisius	Min	FG M-A	FT M-A	Reb O-T	A	TP
McCarthy	9	0-0	0-0	0-0	2	0
Seymour	20	1-6	3-4	1-4	0	5
Dyall	32	4-12	2-4	1-4	0	10
Johnson	14	0-1	2-2	1-1	3	2
Book	36	5-14	1-2	2-6	1	11
Brown	25	2-6	0-0	1-1	3	4
James	30	7-13	0-0	1-3	2	16
Ralph Tirado	1	0-0	0-0	0-0	0	0
Wise	22	4-10	1-2	4-6	3	10
Ray Tirado	1	0-0	0-0	0-0	0	0
McCaffrey	3	1-1	0-1	1-1	0	2
Gregory	2	0-1	0-0	0-0	0	0
Sandel	5	0-2	0-0	0-0	1	0
Totals	200	24-66	9-15	16-31	15	60

Duke	47	49	96
Canisius	25	35	60

FG Pct: Duke 66.7, Canisius 36.4
FT Pct: Duke 77.8, Canisius 60.0
3FG Shooting: Duke 4-7 (T. Hill 2-3, Hurley 1-2, Clark 1-1, Laettner 0-1); Canisius 3-9 (James 2-5, Wise 1-2, Seymour 0-1, Brown 0-1)
Turnovers: Duke 23, Canisius 22
Blocks: Duke 6 (Laettner 3), Canisius 2
Steals: Duke 8 (Hill, Hill 2), Canisius 12
Fouled Out: None
Officials: Higgins, Elliott, Donato
Attendance: 16,279

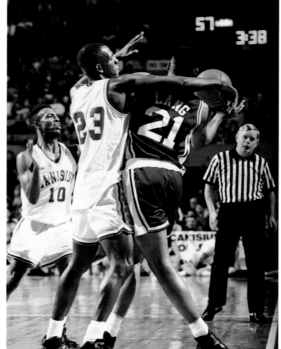

HARRY SCULL

where dreams begin

The making of the annual Duke basketball poster has become one of the team highlights over the years and 1992 was no exception. This year, the team gathered in October at a Durham grade school playground and around 20 area kids were involved through the Durham Parks and Recreation program. Another successful poster and a lot of fun for everyone.

CHUCK LIDDY

They came out wearing gold uniforms in the Fab Five's first national television appearance. Their familiar fight song "Hail to the Victors" was played in Crisler Arena as often as the National Anthem on the Fourth of July. And on this same day Desmond Howard received the coveted Heisman Trophy in New York. It all seemed like a fairy-tale for Michigan faithful until **Bobby Hurley** stepped up and saved the day for top-ranked Duke. In succession, the Jersey City, NJ, native popped a three-pointer with Duke down five at the 1:28 mark and then canned three straight free throws to tie the game with 31.9 seconds left in regulation. All around him was some of the wildest basketball played all season long with an intentional foul, a minor injury, two forced timeout calls, two jump balls and a total of five Hurley free throws. This, after Duke led by as many as 17 points and held a comfortable 56-43 lead early in the second half.

The game was frenetic from the opening tip between All-America **Christian Laettner** and freshman sensation **Chris Webber**. Laettner finished the game with 24 points while Webber had 27 to lead Michigan. Both players fouled out in the extra period. Interestingly, the winning team in the 1989 and 1991 meetings of Duke and Michigan became the eventual national champion in college basketball. Little did anyone know that that streak would not only hold true in 1992 but the two would also meet again 113 days later for the title.

"

We were just like two dogs in a dogfight going at it. It seems like we were in a corner most of the time. We didn't let them bite our necks, though. We just kept fighting. And they just finally took the breath out of us.
– *Chris Webber*

BRIAN SPURLOCK

BRIAN SPURLOCK

December 14, 1991
Crisler Arena, Ann Arbor, MI

Duke	Min	FG M-A	FT M-A	Reb O-T	A	TP
G. Hill	31	6-9	4-5	1-6	0	16
Davis	43	5-12	2-3	4-7	0	12
Laettner	37	6-9	11-12	1-8	1	24
Hurley	45	6-13	12-14	1-2	7	26
T. Hill	38	3-9	0-0	1-3	1	6
Lang	17	1-4	0-0	1-1	0	2
Clark	9	0-1	2-2	0-0	0	2
Meek	5	0-0	0-0	0-1	0	0
Totals	225	27-57	31-36	10-31	9	88

Michigan	Min	FG M-A	FT M-A	Reb O-T	A	TP
Webber	39	11-15	4-6	7-12	3	27
Voskuil	33	5-8	0-0	1-3	1	11
Howard	33	1-5	2-2	2-8	2	4
Rose	36	7-14	4-4	1-4	6	18
Talley	28	3-8	0-0	1-2	2	6
King	32	5-10	2-3	1-3	0	15
Riley	17	1-3	2-4	1-3	0	4
Hunter	3	0-0	0-0	0-0	0	0
Jackson	3	0-0	0-1	0-0	0	0
Pelinka	1	0-1	0-0	0-0	0	0
Totals	225	33-64	14-20	14-37	14	85

Duke	43	33	12	88
Michigan	33	43	9	85

FG Pct: Duke 47.4, Michigan 51.6
FT Pct: Duke 86.1, Michigan 70.0
3FG Shooting: Duke 3-10 (Hurley 2-6, Laettner 1-2, T. Hill 0-1, Clark 0-1); Michigan 5-9 (King 3-3, Webber 1-2, Voskuil 1-2, Rose 0-1, Pelinka 0-1).
Turnovers: Duke 17, Michigan 21.
Blocks: Duke 0, Michigan 8.
Steals: Duke 7 (Davis, Hurley 2), Michigan 2.
Fouled Out: Laettner, Webber, Talley.
Officials: Paparo, Scagliotta, Croft.
Attendance: 13,609.

CHRIS BARRY

Duke athletic trainer Dave Engelhardt, shown here with co-captain Brian Davis, joined the team in Ann Arbor after veteran Max Crowder was diagnosed with lung cancer shortly before the trip. The game broke a streak of 899 straight games worked by Crowder, dating back to his days as a Duke undergraduate in 1962. Michigan served as the bookends for Engelhardt's season – his first game in December and the team's last game for the national title.

After an unprecedented 16-day layoff for Christmas, Duke returned home to face former Duke assistant coach Chuck Swenson's William & Mary Tribe. The relaxing break didn't faze Duke's competitiveness as the Blue Devils rushed out to a 52-25 halftime advantage in crushing the visitors 97-61. Coach K used a "big" lineup with **Cherokee Parks** reinserted to give him some added confidence. The **Christian Laettner**-Parks combo was impossible for the shorter Tribe to handle as Laettner tallied 25 points, including 21 in the first half while Parks added 10. **Bobby Hurley** had 12 assists for his first double-figure assist total in 1991-92 and the 17th in his career. **Brian Davis** and **Grant Hill** also displayed their dunking abilities for the sellout crowd in Cameron.

"

I thought we played very well. We were efficient at taking advantage of Laettner inside and Bobby played a phenomenal floor game, but we kept a pretty good level of performance throughout the game. The bench gave us good contributions and there wasn't a dropoff in effort from any of our players.
– *Mike Krzyzewski*

CHUCK LIDDY

December 30, 1991
Cameron Indoor Stadium, Durham, NC

William & Mary	Min	FG M-A	FT M-A	Reb O-T	A	TP
Roberts	30	7-13	2-2	2-7	0	17
Blocker	23	2-3	1-2	2-8	0	5
Smith	30	4-13	1-2	1-3	2	9
Connor	31	5-9	0-2	0-1	4	12
Peters	22	2-4	2-3	0-2	0	6
Cox	12	0-3	0-0	0-0	2	0
Cauthorn	15	1-4	0-3	1-2	1	2
Small	11	1-3	3-4	1-1	0	5
Duff	12	2-6	0-0	0-1	0	5
Wakefield	4	0-1	0-0	0-0	0	0
Purpura	2	0-0	0-0	0-1	0	0
Payton	7	0-0	0-0	0-0	0	0
Dux	1	0-0	0-0	0-0	0	0
Totals	200	24-59	9-18	12-33	9	61

Duke	Min	FG M-A	FT M-A	Reb O-T	A	TP
Davis	25	1-7	0-0	0-2	1	2
Laettner	21	10-13	4-5	3-8	2	25
Parks	21	4-8	2-2	1-2	1	10
Hurley	27	4-6	3-4	0-3	12	13
G. Hill	23	4-10	3-4	3-6	3	11
Lang	20	3-7	1-1	2-3	0	7
T. Hill	25	5-7	3-4	0-1	0	13
Clark	13	1-1	0-0	1-1	2	3
Meek	10	1-2	7-7	0-1	0	9
Blakeney	8	0-1	1-2	0-1	0	1
Ast	4	1-2	1-4	1-3	0	3
Burt	3	0-0	0-0	0-0	1	0
Totals	200	34-64	25-33	12-34	22	97

William & Mary	25	36	61
Duke	52	45	97

FG Pct: William & Mary 40.7, Duke 53.1
FT Pct: William & Mary 50.0, Duke 75.8
3FG Shooting: W&M 4-10 (Connor 2-2, Roberts 1-2, Duff 1-3, Cox 0-3); Duke 4-12 (Hurley 2-4, Laettner 1-2, Clark 1-1, Davis 0-2, T. Hill 0-1, Blakeney 0-1, Ast 0-1).
Turnovers: William & Mar 20, Duke 9.
Blocks: William & Mary 2, Duke 5 (Laettner 2)
Steals: William & Mary 3, Duke 11 (several 2)
Fouled Out: None
Officials: Wirtz, Gordon, Scott
Attendance: 9,314

January 2, 1992
University Hall, Charlottesville, VA

Duke	Min	FG M-A	FT M-A	Reb O-T	A	TP
G. Hill	31	6-9	4-4	0-3	4	16
Parks	11	0-1	3-4	2-4	0	3
Laettner	30	7-12	2-3	4-9	1	17
Hurley	35	2-12	6-6	0-1	8	11
Davis	30	1-5	0-0	1-2	0	2
T. Hill	32	5-12	0-0	3-6	1	12
Lang	20	2-3	1-3	0-2	0	5
Clark	11	1-1	0-0	0-0	1	2
Totals	200	24-55	16-20	13-31	15	68

Virginia	Min	FG M-A	FT M-A	Reb O-T	A	TP
Burrough	33	4-10	3-7	5-11	2	11
Stith	35	7-15	1-1	0-4	1	17
Jeffries	33	2-6	0-0	2-5	2	4
Oliver	18	3-8	0-0	1-2	1	6
Alexander	36	5-12	0-0	1-4	7	13
Smith	9	1-1	2-2	0-1	2	4
Parker	27	2-3	0-0	2-4	1	5
Wilson	2	0-2	0-0	1-1	0	0
Barnes	7	1-1	0-0	1-3	0	2
Totals	200	25-58	6-10	15-37	16	62

Duke	41	27	68
Virginia	37	25	62

FG Pct: Duke 43.6, Virginia 43.1
FT Pct: Duke 80.0, Virginia 60.0
3FG Shooting: Duke 4-15 (T. Hill 2-5, Laettner 1-2, Hurley 1-8); Virginia 6-12 (Alexander 3-5, Stith 2-3, Parker 1-2, Oliver 0-2).
Turnovers: Duke 14, Virginia 20
Blocks: Duke 1 (Laettner), Virginia 1
Steals: Duke 7 (G. Hill, Laettner 2), Virginia 2
Fouled Out: None
Officials: Paparo, Edsall, Hartzell
Attendance: 8,864

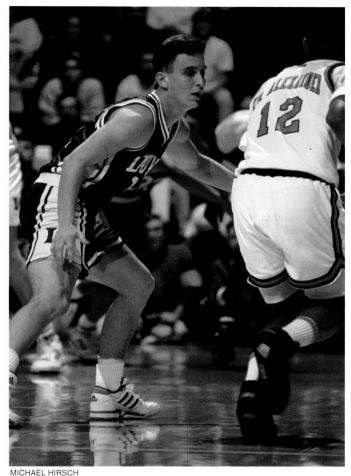

MICHAEL HIRSCH

Ahead by just two points (61-59) with 26 seconds remaining in the game and three seconds on the shot clock, Mr. Clutch **Bobby Hurley** delivered again for the Blue Devils. Hurley, who had made just one of 11 shots at that point in the game, knocked down a three-pointer to put the game out of reach for the Cavaliers and hand Duke its seventh consecutive win, 68-62.

Duke never led by more than nine points the entire game in Charlottesville but **Grant Hill** was a key to victory with 16 points and four assists. His four points in a 10-0 Duke run midway through the second half wiped out Virginia's only lead of the game at 44-43.

> Things change at ACC time. I expect every road game in the ACC to be like this one. Teams know each other. When you get in the ACC, it's not a matter of X's and O's. It's a matter of who wants it.
> *– Grant Hill*

January 6, 1992
Cameron Indoor Stadium, Durham, NC

Florida State	Min	FG M-A	FT M-A	Reb O-T	A	TP
Edwards	34	2-14	3-3	4-6	2	7
Sura	35	5-8	7-10	2-2	2	19
Dobard	25	2-4	0-1	2-8	1	4
Graham	18	4-7	0-0	0-0	0	10
Cassell	33	9-18	2-2	1-1	4	20
Ward	30	1-7	2-2	1-3	3	4
Reid	21	1-4	0-0	2-6	0	2
Donald	4	2-2	0-0	0-0	0	4
Totals	200	26-64	14-18	13-28	12	70

Duke	Min	FG M-A	FT M-A	Reb O-T	A	TP
G. Hill	34	10-12	6-7	1-10	1	26
Davis	27	7-11	5-5	5-9	6	19
Laettner	26	7-12	2-2	1-5	0	16
Hurley	37	1-8	5-6	0-1	8	7
T. Hill	27	4-6	2-3	0-4	2	11
Clark	11	0-2	0-0	0-1	0	0
Lang	22	1-3	3-4	3-5	3	5
Meek	5	0-0	1-2	0-1	0	1
Parks	7	0-1	1-2	1-1	0	1
Blakeney	4	0-2	0-1	3-3	0	0
Totals	200	30-57	25-32	15-41	20	86

Florida State	24	46	70
Duke	42	44	86

FG Pct: Florida State 40.6, Duke 52.6
FT Pct: Florida State 77.7, Duke 78.1
3FG Shooting: Florida State 4-13 (Sura 2-3, Graham 2-3, Cassell 0-3, Edwards 0-3, Ward 0-1); Duke 1-9 (T. Hill 1-3, Hurley 0-4, Laettner, 0-1, Clark 0-1).
Turnovers: Florida State 24, Duke 23
Blocks: Florida State 4, Duke 7 (G. Hill 4)
Steals: Florida State 11, Duke 12 (G. Hill 5)
Fouled Out: Reid.
Officials: Wirtz, Gray, Lembo
Attendance: 9,314

CHUCK LIDDY

Grant Hill and **Brian Davis** had career scoring highs with 26 and 19 points, respectively, in Florida State's initial visit to Cameron Indoor Stadium as a member of the Atlantic Coast Conference. And like their fellow brethren of the ACC, the Seminoles went home losers to the nation's top-ranked team. The final score was 86-70 but Duke held a 25-point second half lead at 66-41 with 8:21 to play. The game featured an unpredictable pace and few jump shots as the Seminoles dictated the pace with their frenetic all-court style. Duke's athleticism won out though, as Hill made 10-of-12 shots, including four rim-rattling dunks and Davis was 7-of-11 from the field to go with his nine rebounds and six assists.

> I'll tell you one thing - I didn't realize how fast they were. They flat outran our kids down the floor. Right now, we're slow getting back in transition, but they run the wings and attack the basket as well as anybody.
> *– Pat Kennedy*
> *Florida State coach*

Duke claimed its ninth consecutive win over Maryland and the 15th in the past 16 meetings with a decisive 83-66 win in College Park. The Blue Devils quickly built a 25-8 lead, making 12 of their first 16 shots of the game, to open a working margin the entire contest. Holding a 41-28 halftime lead, **Thomas Hill** sparked the Blue Devils to a 10-0 run to start the second half with a three-pointer just six seconds into the frame. A sparkling transition layup by **Bobby Hurley** made it 51-28 and sent significant portions of a sold out Cole Field House home. Duke's tenacious defense forced Maryland into 24 turnovers, including 11 by All-America Walt Williams. Also of note was Hurley setting a new school standard for career three-pointers with his 129th in the game.

Brian Davis, a native of Capitol Heights, MD, played before the "home" crowd one last time. **Marty Clark** and **Ron Burt** helped seal Duke's 9-0 record.

It was our best effort of the year. It was like a tournament game in that we were very, very intense.
– *Brian Davis*

I took what the defense gave me. If you miss, you tell yourself you'll hit the next one. We were struggling just a little bit with our outside shots, but tonight we had confidence in it.
– *Thomas Hill*

January 8, 1992
Cole Field House, College Park, MD

Duke	Min	FG M-A	FT M-A	Reb O-T	A	TP
G. Hill	31	4-11	3-6	2-6	6	11
Davis	25	2-6	0-0	0-3	4	4
Laettner	33	4-8	4-8	2-7	2	13
Hurley	29	3-7	0-0	0-1	6	9
T. Hill	30	9-16	4-6	5-8	2	25
Lang	18	1-3	1-2	3-5	1	3
Clark	11	2-2	0-0	0-1	2	5
Parks	9	2-4	4-6	2-3	1	8
Blakeney	6	0-0	0-0	0-0	0	0
Meek	4	2-3	1-4	1-1	0	5
Burt	2	0-2	0-0	0-0	0	0
Ast	2	0-0	0-0	0-2	0	0
Totals	200	29-62	17-32	18-43	24	83

Maryland	Min	FG M-A	FT M-A	Reb O-T	A	TP
Smith	29	4-16	0-2	3-7	1	8
Broadnax	29	1-6	2-2	1-1	2	4
Burns	26	3-4	0-0	0-3	0	6
McLinton	39	7-14	3-3	0-3	7	19
Williams	34	8-17	6-8	5-7	0	25
Kerwin	26	1-1	0-0	2-8	1	2
Downing	5	0-0	0-0	0-0	0	0
Bristol	8	1-2	0-0	1-2	1	2
Soto	2	0-0	0-2	1-1	0	0
Horton	1	0-1	0-0	0-0	0	0
Walsh	1	0-1	0-0	1-2	0	0
Totals	200	25-62	11-17	15-36	12	66

Duke	41	42	83
Maryland	28	38	66

FG Pct: Duke 46.8, Maryland 40.3
FT Pct: Duke 53.1, Maryland 64.7
3FG Shooting: Duke 8-12 (T. Hill 3-5, Hurley 3-5, Clark 1-1, Laettner 1-1); Maryland 5-13 (Williams 3-6, McLinton 2-4, Smith 0-2, Horton 0-1).
Turnovers: Duke 19, Maryland 24
Blocks: Duke 3 (three with 1), Maryland 4
Steals: Duke 8 (T. Hill, Laettner 2), Maryland 4
Fouled Out: Davis, Hurley, Williams, Kerwin
Officials: Rose, Higgins, Pitts
Attendance: 14,500

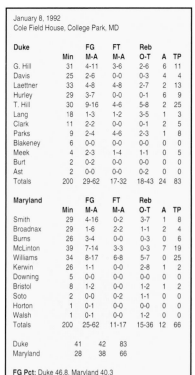

MICHAEL HIRSCH

BOB DONNAN

The scene was set: the collision of the last two unbeaten ACC teams and the return of the Cameron Crazies from the holiday break. The result was predictable: Duke 97, Georgia Tech 84. And the usual suspects were up to the task of giving Duke the decisive win. All-America **Christian Laettner** was spectacular in scoring 33 points and grabbing 11 rebounds in his first double-double of the season; playmaker extraordinare **Bobby Hurley** ran circles around the Jackets with 17 points, 12 assists, 3-of-3 three-point attempts, and committed just two turnovers in 36 minutes; and don't forget **Grant Hill** who showed superb defense like this block of Malcolm Mackey's shot.

"

Christian played like a maniac. He was a hundred percent today. He goes after people and nobody can stop him. He just took his game to another level. You can see it in his eyes. He wants the ball, he passes the ball very well, and he's in focus to play better than anybody on the court. He was awesome.
– Bobby Hurley

January 11, 1992
Cameron Indoor Stadium, Durham, NC

Georgia Tech	Min	FG M-A	FT M-A	Reb O-T	A	TP
Mackey	39	7-12	2-6	5-10	2	16
Forrest	32	6-13	2-2	2-4	1	14
Geiger	17	2-3	3-4	0-1	1	7
Best	33	6-10	1-2	0-1	6	15
Barry	38	11-20	2-2	3-6	3	28
Newbill	24	0-3	0-0	2-4	1	0
Hill	10	1-5	0-0	1-1	0	2
Vinson	7	1-4	0-0	0-0	1	2
Totals	200	34-70	10-16	14-28	15	84

Duke	Min	FG M-A	FT M-A	Reb O-T	A	TP
G. Hill	30	5-7	2-2	2-6	2	12
Davis	28	5-7	4-6	4-9	1	14
Laettner	31	15-19	2-5	5-11	2	33
Hurley	36	6-13	2-2	0-1	12	17
T. Hill	29	6-13	0-0	1-2	3	13
Lang	17	0-2	0-1	2-2	2	0
Clark	11	2-3	0-0	1-1	2	4
Parks	13	2-4	0-0	0-2	1	4
Blakeney	2	0-0	0-0	0-0	0	0
Meek	2	0-1	0-0	0-0	1	0
Ast	1	0-0	0-0	0-0	0	0
Totals	200	41-69	10-16	17-38	26	97

Georgia Tech	41	43	84
Duke	48	49	97

FG Pct: Georgia Tech 48.6, Duke 59.4
FT Pct: Georgia Tech 62.5, Duke 62.5
3FG Shooting: Georgia Tech 6-15 (Barry 4-10, Best 2-4, Vinson 0-1); Duke 5-7 (Hurley 3-3, T. Hill 1-3, Laettner 1-1).
Turnovers: Georgia Tech 13, Duke 14
Blocks: Georgia Tech 6, Duke 1 (G. Hill)
Steals: Georgia Tech 7, Duke 7 (Laettner 3)
Fouled Out: Geiger
Officials: Hartzell, Croft, Rote
Attendance: 9,314

The Blue Devils were hot-shooting from the outset and turned it up a notch higher in the second half as Duke claimed its most lopsided victory over N.C. State since 1967 with a 110-75 win. Duke shot 63.6 percent for the game from the field and 67.6 in the second half in using easy shots such as **Grant Hill's** layup to crush the Wolfpack in Cameron. Coach K praised the entire team for a great effort as **Bobby Hurley** was solid with 19 points, 10 assists and six rebounds while **Christian Laettner** matched up well against Tom Gugliotta for the last time in Durham. Laettner had 23 points to Gugs' 22. **Thomas Hill** showed superb defense and scored 19 points as 10 Duke players scored in the game, including freshman **Erik Meek** who contributed four points and three rebounds in seven minutes of action.

"

I just think we can turn up the intensity every once in a while to super-high. Throughout the game, we're doing a good job of being intense, but every once in a while, we'll get a run going.
– Christian Laettner

CHUCK LIDDY

January 15, 1992
Cameron Indoor Stadium, Durham, NC

N.C. State	Min	FG M-A	FT M-A	Reb O-T	A	TP
Gugliotta	32	10-20	0-1	1-7	1	22
Davis	15	1-2	1-2	1-1	0	3
Thompson	29	5-10	1-2	4-6	1	11
Seale	34	6-9	1-1	1-3	9	14
Bakali	23	0-4	2-2	0-2	1	2
Marshall	29	3-6	1-2	0-1	2	9
Knox	16	2-2	1-2	1-3	0	5
Newman	11	3-5	0-1	1-3	0	8
Lewis	7	0-1	0-0	0-1	0	0
Fletcher	2	0-0	0-0	0-0	0	0
Robinson	2	0-1	1-2	0-0	1	1
Totals	200	30-60	8-15	9-28	15	75

Duke	Min	FG M-A	FT M-A	Reb O-T	A	TP
Davis	28	2-5	3-4	0-0	1	7
G. Hill	31	6-9	3-4	1-4	4	15
Laettner	23	9-12	3-3	3-6	1	23
Hurley	31	7-12	1-3	2-6	10	19
T. Hill	29	8-11	0-0	0-3	3	19
Clark	14	2-2	1-2	1-2	2	6
Lang	12	1-1	3-4	1-4	1	5
Parks	17	3-6	2-3	0-3	1	8
Meek	7	2-5	0-0	0-3	0	4
Blakeney	5	2-3	0-0	0-1	0	4
Ast	2	0-0	0-0	0-0	0	0
Burt	1	0-0	0-0	0-0	1	0
Totals	200	42-66	16-23	10-34	24	110

Wake Forest	37	38	75
Duke	48	62	110

FG Pct: N.C. State 50.0, Duke 63.6
FT Pct: N.C. State 53.3, Duke 69.6
3FG Shooting: N.C. State 7-15 (Marshall 2-3, Newman 2-3, Gugliotta 2-5, Seale 1-1, Bakali 0-3); Duke 10-15 (Hurley 4-6, T. Hill 3-5, Laettner 2-3, Clark 1-1).
Turnovers: N.C. State 19, Duke 12
Blocks: N.C. State 4, Duke 3 (Parks 3)
Steals: N.C. State 9, Duke 9 (Hurley 4)
Fouled Out: Davis
Officials: Paparo, Edsall, Gordon
Attendance: 9,314

BOB DONNAN

CHUCK LIDDY

UNC Charlotte and head coach Jeff Mullins returned to Cameron Indoor Stadium for the second straight season and left again knowing they had given a supreme effort that would have resulted in a win at most places. But the top-ranked Blue Devils were up to the task of the hungry and 18th-ranked 49ers as **Thomas Hill** hit 10-of-12 shots and scored 23 points in the 104-82 win. Duke never trailed in the game as the Blue Devils committed just seven turnovers and **Grant Hill** made all five of his field goal attempts, including this nice dunk. The Duke fans welcomed the 49ers with a chant of, "OVer-RAted, OVer-RAted" as Duke opened a quick 7-0 lead but the game never did feature a blowout of the eventual NCAA Tournament-bound 49ers. Duke led by just 10 at the half when **Christian Laettner** sparked the Blue Devils with a three-point play and Thomas Hill knocked down three straight jumpers for a 66-47 lead with 14:04 to play.

"

I thought I was playing with Johnny Dawkins for a little bit. He really had an excellent game. When we see he is hot like that, we're going to keep going to him. He's a powerful player. He gets so high on his shot, and he shoots it so well.

– *Grant Hill*
on teammate Thomas Hill

January 18, 1992
Cameron Indoor Stadium, Durham, NC

UNC Charlotte	Min	FG M-A	FT M-A	Reb O-T	A	TP
Dottin	25	6-9	3-7	6-8	0	15
Wylie	16	1-2	0-0	1-3	2	3
Odom	38	6-14	0-3	2-4	2	12
Williams	36	8-15	2-2	0-1	3	22
Terrell	31	9-15	0-0	0-1	4	23
Johnson	26	2-5	0-0	0-4	4	5
DeVaull	10	0-2	0-0	0-1	0	0
Bolly	7	0-0	0-0	0-2	0	0
Broadhurst	11	1-1	0-0	0-0	2	2
Totals	200	33-63	5-12	12-29	17	82

Duke	Min	FG M-A	FT M-A	Reb O-T	A	TP
Davis	28	3-5	4-4	1-5	1	10
G. Hill	24	5-5	2-2	0-1	1	12
Laettner	30	8-14	7-7	0-6	1	24
Hurley	36	4-9	0-0	0-2	11	8
T. Hill	32	10-12	2-3	1-3	1	23
Lang	22	3-6	5-6	3-5	0	11
Clark	11	3-5	0-0	1-2	1	8
Parks	14	3-6	2-2	1-2	0	8
Meek	1	0-1	0-0	0-1	0	0
Blakeney	1	0-1	0-0	0-0	0	0
Burt	1	0-0	0-0	0-0	0	0
Totals	200	39-64	22-24	9-30	16	104

UNC Charlotte	39	43	82
Duke	49	55	104

FG Pct: UNC Charlotte 52.4, Duke 60.9
FT Pct: UNC Charlotte 41.7, Duke 91.7
3FG Shooting: UNCC 11-18 (Terrell 5-8, Williams 4-6, Wylie 1-2, Johnson 1-1, Odom 0-1); Duke 4-14 (Clark 2-4, T. Hill 1-3, Laettner 1-2, Davis 0-2, Hurley 0-2, Blakeney 0-1).
Turnovers: UNC Charlotte 14, Duke 7
Blocks: UNC Charlotte 1, Duke 4 (four players)
Steals: UNC Charlotte 1, Duke 7 (Laettner, T. Hill 2)
Fouled Out: None.
Officials: Moreau, Rose, Wood
Attendance: 9,314

CHUCK LIDDY

Duke	Min	FG M-A	FT M-A	Reb O-T	A	TP
G. Hill	24	6-9	0-1	3-4	2	12
Davis	24	6-9	0-1	3-4	2	12
Laettner	29	5-11	15-20	3-7	0	25
Hurley	29	4-9	6-9	2-3	3	15
T. Hill	29	5-11	0-2	3-6	1	12
Lang	19	0-2	3-7	1-2	1	3
Clark	10	0-3	0-0	0-1	0	0
Parks	17	2-5	4-6	2-3	0	8
Meek	7	0-1	3-4	0-1	0	3
Blakeney	5	0-0	3-4	0-1	0	3
Burt	1	0-0	0-0	0-0	0	0
Totals	200	28-62	36-55	19-39	13	95

Boston U.	Min	FG M-A	FT M-A	Reb O-T	A	TP
Daly	29	4-15	2-2	0-2	6	13
Delgardo	32	6-17	2-2	1-5	3	16
Huckeby	16	2-4	1-2	3-5	0	5
Scott	34	14-16	2-3	5-9	2	30
Roso-Myles	13	0-0	2-2	1-1	1	2
Harris	13	2-4	0-0	1-2	5	4
Wallace	17	2-2	0-0	0-0	3	5
Price	17	2-4	0-0	1-3	0	4
Jarvis	11	0-1	2-2	0-2	5	2
Westerfield	8	0-0	1-2	3-4	0	1
Storm	7	0-1	1-2	2-5	1	1
Manolopoulos	3	0-1	2-2	0-1	0	2
Totals	200	32-65	14-18	17-39	26	85

Duke	46	49	95
Boston U.	33	52	85

FG Pct: Duke 45.2, Boston U. 49.2
FT Pct: Duke 65.5, Boston U. 77.8
3FG Shooting: Duke 3-10 (T. Hill 2-5, Hurley 1-5); Boston U. 6-20 (Daly 3-10, Delgardo 2-5, Wallace 1-1, Huckeby 0-1, Harris 0-1, Price 0-1, Manolopoulos 0-1).
Turnovers: Duke 16, Boston U. 29
Blocks: Duke 1 (Parks), Boston U. 3
Steals: Duke 14 (Hurley, G. Hill 3), Boston U. 7
Fouled Out: Davis, Roso-Myles, Harris, Price
Officials: Mannon, Monjio, Mingle
Attendance: 4,108 (arena record)

January 21, 1992
Brown Arena, Boston, MA

Christian Laettner scored 25 points and top-ranked Duke drew 36 fouls which resulted in 55 free throw attempts to down Boston University 95-85 and push its record to 13-0. Duke had a 24-point lead, 85-61, with 7:45 left but the Terriers fought back with a 24-9 run capped by Mark Daly's three-pointer to cut the lead to 94-85 with 19 seconds left. Christian Laettner converted 15-of-20 free throws, including all 10 in the first half, to lead Duke with 25 points and seven rebounds. All five Duke starters scored in double-figures but BU's Jason Scott took game honors with 30 points on 14-of-16 shooting from the field.

"

It was a very good game for us. There were a lot of lessons learned, a lot of teaching points. To their credit, they put us in that position. All those kids played so hard because they played like they have nothing to lose.
– Mike Krzyzewski

Wake Forest	Min	FG M-A	FT M-A	Reb O-T	A	TP
King	31	6-11	0-2	1-3	1	12
Rogers	35	8-18	2-5	4-7	2	18
Medlin	26	1-4	2-2	2-7	2	4
Tucker	31	1-3	2-2	0-3	4	4
McQueen	33	4-7	2-2	0-1	4	11
Owens	22	2-7	2-2	0-1	0	6
Doggett	12	4-7	2-2	0-0	0	11
Banks	2	0-1	0-0	0-0	0	0
Hicks	5	1-2	0-0	3-5	0	2
Llewellyn	2	0-0	0-0	0-0	0	0
Blucas	1	0-0	0-0	0-0	0	0
Totals	200	27-60	12-17	12-30	13	68

Duke	Min	FG M-A	FT M-A	Reb O-T	A	TP
Davis	34	4-9	2-3	0-7	0	10
G. Hill	31	7-10	2-2	1-6	6	16
Laettner	30	10-15	2-2	2-5	1	25
Hurley	30	3-5	5-5	0-4	10	12
T. Hill	26	5-8	0-0	0-0	1	11
Lang	21	2-2	0-2	2-2	3	4
Parks	18	2-4	0-0	0-1	0	4
Clark	6	1-2	0-0	0-1	0	2
Blakeney	3	0-0	0-0	0-1	2	0
Meek	1	0-0	0-0	0-0	0	0
Totals	200	34-55	11-14	5-28	23	84

Wake Forest	34	34	68
Duke	45	39	84

FG Pct: Wake Forest 45.0, Duke 61.8
FT Pct: Wake Forest 70.6, Duke 78.6
3FG Shooting: Wake 2-6 (Doggett 1-2, McQueen 1-1, King 0-1, Owens 0-1, Banks 0-1); Duke 5-8 (Laettner 3-4, Hurley 1-1, T. Hill 1-1, Davis 0-2).
Turnovers: Wake Forest 17, Duke 16
Blocks: Wake Forest 0, Duke 6 (Davis 2)
Steals: Wake Forest 8, Duke 5 (Lang 2)
Fouled Out: None
Officials: Wirtz, Scagliotta, Gray
Attendance: 9,314

January 25, 1992
Cameron Indoor Stadium, Durham, NC

CHUCK LIDDY

Duke ripped into its 14th straight victim with a stupendous second half defense and accurate shooting throughout the game in upending Wake Forest 84-68 before a national CBS audience. The Blue Devils led just 49-41 with 15:36 to play when Mike Krzyzewski called timeout to lecture his team about defense. His team responded with a patented 27-8 run which featured a balanced attack by all five starters. **Christian Laettner** started it off with six straight points, followed by a **Brian Davis** jumper, a **Thomas Hill** drive, a **Bobby Hurley** left-handed layup, and a **Grant Hill** open jumper. Cool, calculating and deadly was the Duke attack as all five finished in double-figures and Duke won its eighth straight at home.

"

Duke's defense had a lot to do with my missed shots and so did Cameron Indoor Stadium. It's hard enough to beat Duke without playing them here.
– Rodney Rogers

Christian Laettner scored his 2,000th career point and eight Duke players scored in double-figures as the Blue Devils fast breaked Clemson to death 112-73. The Blue Devil defense was punishing as it forced 23 Tiger turnovers and converted that into 38 points, including 25 in the first half. **Cherokee Parks** led all scorers with a career-high 19 points off the bench. In fact, the Duke bench contributed 50 points and 22 rebounds in the game. **Marty Clark** added 11 points while **Kenny Blakeney** played 11 minutes. The Blue Devils shot 71.9 percent from the field in the second half to add to a 55-27 halftime advantage. Duke's biggest lead was 43 points at 76-33 while Laettner became the 27th player in ACC history with 2,000 or more career points. The win gave Duke a 7-0 record in the ACC, its best start since 1964.

"

We run an unstructured fast break to take advantage of our guys' ability to handle and catch the ball. When we get a turnover, we don't pick it up and hold it. If our guys can't get it to Bobby Hurley right away, they can push it up the floor themselves.
– *Mike Krzyzewski*

January 27, 1992
Cameron Indoor Stadium, Durham, NC

Clemson	Min	FG M-A	FT M-A	Reb O-T	A	TP
Harris	30	6-9	2-2	2-6	5	14
Hines	24	2-4	0-0	2-3	1	4
Wright	22	3-11	0-0	2-5	0	6
Burks	18	1-4	0-0	0-0	0	2
Whitney	21	1-4	0-0	0-2	2	2
Bovain	8	2-3	0-0	0-1	0	5
Wallace	27	3-9	0-1	3-5	1	6
Gray	21	10-11	2-5	2-2	1	22
Martin	16	1-3	0-0	0-0	1	3
Amestoy	11	3-7	1-1	0-1	0	7
Smith	2	0-0	2-2	0-0	1	2
Totals	200	32-65	7-11	13-27	12	73

Duke	Min	FG M-A	FT M-A	Reb O-T	A	TP
Davis	19	4-7	3-6	0-0	3	11
G. Hill	22	5-8	0-0	1-5	4	10
Laettner	20	4-6	2-2	2-5	2	11
Hurley	22	5-8	1-1	1-1	6	14
T. Hill	22	7-11	2-3	0-1	2	16
Lang	24	5-7	2-3	3-7	0	12
Parks	24	8-10	3-5	4-8	1	19
Clark	18	5-8	4-4	0-0	0	11
Meek	14	2-3	0-2	3-4	1	4
Blakeney	11	1-2	0-0	0-2	2	2
Burt	4	0-1	2-2	0-1	0	2
Totals	200	44-68	19-28	16-36	21	112

Clemson	27	46	73
Duke	55	57	112

FG Pct: Clemson 49.2, Duke 64.7
FT Pct: Clemson 63.6, Duke 67.9
3FG Shooting: Clemson 2-9 (Bovain 1-2, Martin 1-2, Whitney 0-2, Wallace 0-1, Amestoy 0-1, Burks 0-1; Duke 5-11 (Hurley 3-4, Laettner 1-2, Clark 1-1, Davis 0-2, T. Hill 0-2).
Turnovers: Clemson 23, Duke 15
Blocks: Clemson 1, Duke 6 (Parks 3)
Steals: Clemson 4, Duke 13 (Laettner, T. Hill 4)
Fouled Out: Wright
Officials: Rose, Hartzell, Higgins
Attendance: 9,314

BOB DONNAN

CHUCK LIDDY

BOB DONNAN

PHIL SEARS

The final score, 75-62, looked like another easy Duke win, but with three minutes to play, this game looked like the end of the Blue Devils' unbeaten streak. Duke trailed 62-61 with 3:40 remaining when **Grant Hill** took charge with eight points and a key steal as the Blue Devils rallied with the game's final 14 points for the win. Coach K made a key move at the final TV timeout with 3:14 to go when he switched Hill to cover Sam Cassell who had scored 15 points and hurt Duke with his penetration. After a layup to give Duke the lead, 64-62, Hill extinguished FSU's hopes for good with a breakaway steal and layup for a 67-62 lead with 1:20 to play. Duke continued its tough defensive maneuvers to preserve the win as Hill finished with 20 points and 10 rebounds and **Christian Laettner** had 20 points and nine rebounds. Duke's first ever win in Tallahassee moved the Blue Devils to 16-0 on the season, equaling the best start in school history, and was the 22nd straight victory overall, also a school record.

"

We outplayed them some and they outplayed us some. I thought the last three minutes of the game, our experience of playing together was outstanding. Our guys were terrific in the last three minutes, hitting the free throws, coming up with defensive boards, and Grant Hill making a couple of defensive plays.
– Mike Krzyzewski

January 30, 1992
Tallahassee Civic Auditorium, Tallahassee, FL

Duke	Min	FG M-A	FT M-A	Reb O-T	A	TP
G. Hill	34	7-12	6-7	2-10	2	20
Davis	37	1-4	4-5	4-6	1	7
Laettner	36	5-10	9-12	1-9	0	20
Hurley	40	4-11	0-0	0-1	7	11
T. Hill	33	3-7	1-2	1-3	3	7
Lang	15	3-7	2-3	3-4	0	8
Parks	5	0-0	2-2	0-1	0	2
Totals	200	32-65	7-11	13-27	12	73

Florida State	Min	FG M-A	FT M-A	Reb O-T	A	TP
Cassell	35	7-16	0-0	1-2	5	15
Ward	40	2-7	0-0	0-4	6	4
Edwards	31	4-9	1-1	2-7	5	9
Graham	20	4-10	3-4	2-4	1	12
Dobard	30	6-10	0-3	1-5	0	12
Sura	25	3-6	0-1	0-0	1	6
Reid	19	2-3	0-0	2-4	0	4
Totals	200	28-61	4-9	10-31	18	62

Duke	39	36	75
Florida State	37	25	62

FG Pct: Duke 45.0, Florida State 45.9
FT Pct: Duke 80.0, Florida State 44.4
3FG Shooting: Duke 5-11 (Hurley 3-6, Laettner 1-1, Davis 1-2, T. Hill 0-2); FSU 2-14 (Graham 1-5, Cassell 1-6, Ward 0-1, Edwards 0-1, Sura 0-1).
Turnovers: Duke 20, Florida State 17
Blocks: Duke 3 (Laettner 2), Florida State 6
Steals: Duke 5 (G. Hill 2), Florida State 8
Fouled Out: Cassell
Officials: Paparo, Edsall, Donato
Attendance: 13,610 (new stadium record)

CHUCK LIDDY

duke vs. notre dame

Duke's 500th win in Cameron Indoor Stadium won't go down as one of the most memorable in the history of the building but, nonetheless, it was another cherished blowout in 1991-92, this time over Notre Dame 100-71. The Blue Devils opened a 19-16 lead early in the game and then put the contest out of doubt with an 11-0 run and an insurmountable 51-28 halftime lead. **Christian Laettner** was magnificent with 29 points while hitting 11-of-14 shots. **Thomas Hill** was devastating with his "air"obatics and 14 points. Coach K also cited the play of **Antonio Lang** as his best of the year with his eight points and four rebounds off the bench. **Bobby Hurley** also went over the 1,000 career-point mark with 11 in the game to give him 1,003.

It's great to be a part of history (Duke's 500th win in Cameron). It's something that will be nice to reflect on in 20 years when we all have more weight and less hair.
– *Brian Davis*

KEVIN KEISTER

February 1, 1992
Cameron Indoor Stadium, Durham, NC

Notre Dame

	Min	FG M-A	FT M-A	Reb O-T	A	TP
Ellis	37	7-11	4-4	1-7	1	18
Taylor	24	0-2	0-0	0-2	2	0
Ross, Jon	14	2-4	2-2	0-0	2	6
Bennett	35	5-10	2-2	0-1	6	12
Sweet	34	8-15	2-2	0-2	3	18
Ross, Joe	17	2-2	0-0	0-1	1	4
Cozen	3	0-0	0-0	0-0	0	0
Russell	18	3-3	1-3	1-3	1	7
Boyer	4	1-3	0-0	1-1	0	2
Justice	5	2-2	0-0	0-0	0	4
Gilmore	9	0-2	0-0	0-1	1	0
Totals	200	30-54	11-13	5-19	17	71

Duke

	Min	FG M-A	FT M-A	Reb O-T	A	TP
Davis	31	5-10	2-2	1-2	4	13
G. Hill	28	4-7	3-4	1-6	2	11
Laettner	27	11-14	7-9	4-6	2	29
Hurley	29	3-6	3-4	0-5	7	11
T. Hill	27	5-9	4-4	2-3	3	14
Lang	17	3-5	2-2	4-4	0	8
Parks	22	1-2	3-6	1-4	0	5
Clark	10	2-4	0-0	0-0	0	5
Meek	4	0-2	0-0	1-1	0	0
Blakeney	3	0-0	4-4	0-0	1	4
Burt	2	0-0	0-0	0-0	0	0
Totals	200	39-64	22-24	9-30	16	104

Notre Dame	28	43	71
Duke	51	49	100

FG Pct: Notre Dame 55.6, Duke 57.6
FT Pct: Notre Dame 84.6, Duke 80.0
3FG Shooting: Notre Dame 0-2 (Bennett 0-2); Duke 4-8 (Hurley 2-4, Davis 1-3, Clark 1-1).
Turnovers: Notre Dame 15, Duke 13
Blocks: Notre Dame 4, Duke 3 (three players with 1)
Steals: Notre Dame 4, Duke 7 (Laettner 3)
Fouled Out: Jon Ross
Officials: Parramore, Stockner, Mayborg
Attendance: 9,314

32

BOB DONNAN

The pristine Smith Center rocked and was nearly as loud as nearby Cameron Indoor Stadium . **Bobby Hurley** broke his foot midway through the first half...but played anyway. UNC's Eric Montross and Kevin Salvadori used their seven-foot frames to perfection in dominating the middle on both ends of the court. In the end it all added up to a 75-73 North Carolina upset victory over top-ranked Duke. Twice in the game's final minute, **Christian Laettner** had a chance to tie the score with a jump shot but both attempts trickled off the rim and ended in the hands of the ninth-ranked Tar Heels. His final missed shot, with just seconds remaining, ignited a celebration never before seen in the Smith Center as the students rushed the court and took down the nets. **Brian Davis** led Duke with 17 points.

"

We don't want to say a loss is inevitable. But we think we can lose. And a couple of injuries can change the whole chemistry of the game and you'll lose. Winning every game is not one of our goals; playing as well as we can every game is our main goal.
– Brian Davis
prior to 1991-92 season

February 5, 1992
Smith Center, Chapel Hill, NC

Duke	Min	FG M-A	FT M-A	Reb O-T	A	TP
Davis	37	7-15	2-3	3-5	0	17
G. Hill	37	5-10	0-1	1-3	7	10
Laettner	35	4-11	3-4	6-12	1	12
T. Hill	29	7-11	0-0	2-5	0	16
Hurley	37	3-10	3-6	0-0	6	11
Clark	3	0-1	0-0	0-1	0	0
Lang	14	1-3	1-2	1-4	0	3
Parks	8	0-0	4-4	0-0	0	4
Totals	200	27-61	13-20	14-31	14	73

North Carolina	Min	FG M-A	FT M-A	Reb O-T	A	TP
Reese	20	4-7	1-2	2-3	2	10
Lynch	23	2-9	1-2	1-7	2	5
Montross	28	3-9	6-9	6-9	1	12
Davis	38	5-11	6-6	0-3	1	16
Phelps	35	3-7	2-3	0-3	5	9
Sullivan	20	2-3	2-2	3-3	1	6
Wenstrom	3	0-0	0-0	0-0	0	0
Rodl	9	1-2	0-0	0-1	1	2
Salvadori	22	4-6	4-4	2-6	0	12
Williams	2	1-2	1-1	0-1	0	3
Totals	200	25-56	23-29	14-36	13	75

Duke	39	34	73
North Carolina	38	37	75

FG Pct: Duke 44.3, UNC 44.6
FT Pct: Duke 65.0, UNC 79.3
3FG Shooting: Duke 6-11 (T. Hill 2-2, Hurley 2-6, Laettner 1-2, Davis 1-1); UNC 2-8 (Reese 1-1, Phelps 1-3, Davis 0-3, Sullivan 0-1).
Turnovers: Duke 17, UNC 14
Blocks: Duke 1 (Davis), UNC 6
Steals: Duke 8 (G. Hill, T. Hill 2), UNC 9
Fouled Out: None
Officials: Wirtz, Moreau, Gray
Attendance: 21,572

Minus Bobby Hurley, Duke headed to Baton Rouge for a rematch with Louisiana State and a celebrated second clash between Christian Laettner and Shaquille O'Neal. And for the second straight season, Laettner and his Duke teammates came out on top, this time by a 77-67 score at the Maravich Assembly Center. Facing a hostile environment, Grant Hill was, as Coach K described, "perfectly spectacular" in his first contest as the point guard. Hill tallied 16 points, six assists and nine rebounds against a swarming LSU assault. Even with Hill controlling the point, the game came down to a late duel between the 1992 NBA first round draft choices, Laettner and O'Neal. LSU held leads of 54-49 and 60-59 midway through the second half when Laettner scored 12 of his 22 points in the final 9:06, including a pair of back-breaking three-pointers to put Duke ahead for good at 65-60. The Tigers missed 10 of their final 13 free throws to seal their fate. The Blue Devils seized the moment and reclaimed the nation's number one ranking deep in the Bayou.

"

I hope the fans appreciated what they saw out there. It was a terrific game. It was like an NCAA game...a late NCAA game. The atmosphere reminded me of a Final Four.
– Mike Krzyzewski

BRIAN SPURLOCK

34

February 8, 1992
Maravich Assembly Center, Baton Rouge, LA

Duke

	Min	FG M-A	FT M-A	Reb O-T	A	TP
Lang	31	5-9	2-2	2-5	3	12
Davis	39	4-7	0-0	2-2	1	8
Laettner	40	8-21	4-4	2-10	3	22
T. Hill	33	7-13	1-1	1-5	4	15
G. Hill	40	6-9	4-7	2-9	6	16
Parks	12	1-2	2-2	2-4	2	4
Clark	3	0-0	0-0	0-0	0	0
Blakeney	2	0-0	0-0	0-1	1	0
Totals	200	31-61	13-16	12-38	20	77

Louisiana State

	Min	FG M-A	FT M-A	Reb O-T	A	TP
Pugh	5	0-0	0-0	0-1	1	0
Singleton	39	5-14	3-4	5-12	3	13
O'Neal	38	11-21	3-9	7-12	2	12
Anderson	17	1-3	0-0	0-2	1	3
Ceasar	33	5-12	0-0	2-4	0	14
Brandon	26	3-6	2-2	0-0	3	9
Williamson	15	0-1	0-2	0-0	0	0
Hansen	9	0-2	0-0	0-0	2	0
Marshall	9	0-0	2-2	0-0	0	2
Boudreaux	7	0-1	0-0	0-1	0	0
Hammink	2	0-0	1-2	0-0	0	1
Totals	200	25-60	11-21	14-33	12	67

Duke	34	43	77
Louisiana State	28	39	67

FG Pct: Duke 50.8, LSU 41.7
FT Pct: Duke 81.3, LSU 52.4
3FG Shooting: Duke 2-7 (Laettner 2-4, T. Hill 0-3); LSU 6-18 (Ceasar 4-7, Brandon 1-4, Anderson 1-3, Hansen 0-2, Williamson 0-1, Boudreaux 0-1).
Turnovers: Duke 13, LSU 14
Blocks: Duke 2 (T. Hill, Lang), LSU 11
Steals: Duke 6 (T. Hill, Laettner 2), LSU 6
Fouled Out: T. Hill
Officials: Scagliotta, Edsall, Lembo
Attendance: 13,846

BRIAN SPURLOCK

Duke took to a slower pace against Georgia Tech in Atlanta and came away with the desired results, a methodical 71-62 victory over the Yellow Jackets. The usually quick-paced Devils took their cue from point guard **Grant Hill** and used the clock on most every possession to open a nine-point halftime lead which eventually turned into a 55-38 laugher with under 10 minutes to play. Hill led the way with 20 points, including a thundering alley-oop dunk off a Brian Davis pass in the first half. The dunk was the CNN Sports "Play of the Day" and arguably the best of his 48 dunks in 1991-92. **Thomas Hill** was equally effective with 18 points and five steals and more of his patented stifling defense.

I thought we gutted it out. We played differently than we normally would have played it. We thought we controlled the game and we didn't want to lose control.
– *Mike Krzyzewski*

February 12, 1992
Alexander Memorial Coliseum, Atlanta, GA

Duke	Min	FG M-A	FT M-A	Reb O-T	A	TP
Lang	17	2-2	1-3	1-1	0	5
Davis	36	3-8	5-7	1-5	3	11
Laettner	38	5-13	4-4	2-8	5	15
T. Hill	38	5-9	6-8	1-3	0	18
G. Hill	40	7-11	6-7	1-6	5	20
Clark	3	0-1	0-0	0-0	0	0
Parks	25	1-1	0-0	0-1	1	2
Blakeney	1	0-0	0-0	0-0	0	0
Meek	1	0-0	0-0	0-0	0	0
Burt	1	0-0	0-0	0-0	0	0
Totals	200	23-45	22-29	7-26	14	71

Georgia Tech	Min	FG M-A	FT M-A	Reb O-T	A	TP
Mackey	39	4-7	1-2	4-11	0	9
Forrest	34	8-14	2-3	3-4	3	18
Geiger	26	3-7	1-3	3-8	1	7
Best	31	0-3	0-0	0-1	5	0
Barry	38	9-21	2-2	2-3	5	24
Newbill	15	0-1	1-2	2-3	0	1
B. Hill	15	1-3	1-2	1-1	0	3
Vinson	2	0-0	0-0	0-0	0	0
Totals	200	25-56	8-14	17-35	14	62

Duke	36	35	71
Georgia Tech	27	35	62

FG Pct: Duke 51.1, Georgia Tech 44.6
FT Pct: Duke 75.9, Georgia Tech 57.1
3FG Shooting: Duke 3-7 (T. Hill 2-2, Laettner 1-5); Georgia Tech 4-12 (Barry 4-12).
Turnovers: Duke 13, Georgia Tech 18
Blocks: Duke 6 (T. Hill, G. Hill, Parks 2), Tech 5
Steals: Duke 10 (Laettner, T. Hill 5), Tech 2
Fouled Out: None
Officials: Paparo, Croft, Donato
Attendance: 10,026

PETE CASSABONE

Not since 1986 had Duke won a game in Raleigh, so even as heavy favorites after the 35-point win in January, nothing could be taken for granted. On top of that, this was the fourth and final game of a demanding road swing against an improved N.C. State squad. Twenty points, six assists and six rebounds from point guard **Grant Hill,** however, helped bring the losing streak to an end as the Blue Devils defeated State 71-63 before an ABC audience. Of course Hill didn't do it all as **Thomas Hill** and **Christian Laettner** both added 16 points in the determined team effort. As promised it wasn't easy with State shooting over 50 percent from the field and Tom Gugliotta pouring in 23 points to keep State within reach. The Wolfpack connected on 8-of-16 three-pointers while **Brian Davis** gave the Reynolds crowd a treat with two tomahawk fast break dunks. For Duke it was the 20th victory of the year, the ninth straight season with 20 or more wins.

"

I'm proud I can finally say I've won at State. I don't know why we weren't able to win before. My freshman and sophomore years it was probably because they were better than us, especially at home. Last year we had a chance at the end. This year we used our experience and did a good job in winning.
– Christian Laettner

BOB DONNAN

37

February 16, 1992
Reynolds Coliseum, Raleigh, NC

Duke

	Min	FG M-A	FT M-A	Reb O-T	A	TP
Lang	22	2-3	2-2	1-2	1	6
Davis	36	3-6	2-4	2-4	5	8
Laettner	38	5-9	3-4	0-6	2	16
T. Hill	37	6-12	3-4	0-3	8	16
G. Hill	40	5-12	10-12	1-6	6	20
Blakeney	8	0-0	0-0	0-1	1	0
Parks	7	0-0	0-0	0-2	0	0
Clark	12	1-1	3-4	0-0	0	5
Totals	200	22-43	23-30	7-27	18	71

N.C. State

	Min	FG M-A	FT M-A	Reb O-T	A	TP
Seale	24	2-4	0-2	0-2	2	6
Gugliotta	32	7-14	5-10	0-6	1	23
Thompson	38	6-9	0-1	3-7	3	12
Davis	32	4-8	0-0	3-7	1	10
Marshall	38	3-9	0-0	1-3	6	6
Bakalli	14	3-3	0-0	0-1	1	6
Knox	1	0-0	0-0	0-0	0	0
Lewis	8	0-0	0-0	0-0	1	0
Totals	200	25-48	5-13	8-27	15	63

Duke	36	35	71
N.C. State	31	32	63

FG Pct: Duke 51.2, N.C. State 52.1
FT Pct: Duke 76.7, N.C. State 38.5
3FG Shooting: Duke 4-6 (Laettner 3-3, T. Hill 1-3); NCSU 8-16 (Gugliotta 4-8, Seale 2-2, Davis 2-4, Marshall 0-2).
Turnovers: Duke 13, N.C. State 15
Blocks: Duke 1 (Parks), N.C. State 1
Steals: Duke 9 (T. Hill 4), N.C. State 8
Fouled Out: None
Officials: Wertz, Gray, Rose
Attendance: 12,400

BOB DONNAN

It was last place Maryland against first place Duke but fans would have been hard-pressed to discover which team was which after watching the Blue Devils barely survive in a 91-89 victory. Duke had plenty of chances to put the game away but the Terrapins would have nothing of it. Duke led 70-56 with 15:21 left and it appeared to be yet another blowout but Maryland answered with a 9-0 run and closed the gap to five with 11:58 to play. Duke led 82-74 when All-America and leading scorer Walt Williams fouled out. Surely that was the end, but no. Kevin McLinton then scored nine of his team's final 15 points and actually put Maryland ahead 89-88 with 39 seconds to go. And if not for an **Antonio Lang** tipin of a **Christian Laettner** miss with seconds to play, Duke would have gone home the loser. It was that kind of night. Laettner led all five of Duke's starters in double-figures with 30 points.

"

What a sensational game by Maryland. What an incredible, gutsy performance by their kids and their coaching staff.
– *Mike Krzyzewski*

February 20, 1992
Cameron Indoor Stadium, Durham, NC

Maryland	Min	FG M-A	FT M-A	Reb O-T	A	TP
Burns	36	6-13	0-3	0-5	2	12
Broadnax	36	4-5	3-4	2-3	2	11
Kerwin	32	3-3	0-0	0-1	1	6
McLinton	39	10-14	4-5	1-2	11	25
Williams	30	9-13	5-7	2-6	2	26
Walsh	8	2-2	0-0	0-0	0	5
Downing	13	1-3	0-0	0-0	1	2
Schultz	4	0-1	0-1	0-1	1	0
Bristol	2	1-1	0-0	0-0	0	2
Totals	200	36-55	12-20	8-22	20	89

Duke	Min	FG M-A	FT M-A	Reb O-T	A	TP
Davis	38	5-7	8-10	1-4	4	19
Lang	29	6-7	0-0	3-6	0	12
Laettner	31	11-22	7-10	5-8	2	30
T. Hill	36	4-7	5-7	0-4	2	13
G. Hill	33	7-12	0-0	1-4	6	14
Parks	19	1-2	1-2	1-1	1	3
Blakeney	11	0-1	0-0	0-0	2	0
Meek	2	0-0	0-0	0-0	0	0
Clark	1	0-0	0-0	0-0	0	0
Totals	200	34-58	21-29	11-28	17	91

Maryland	46	43	89
Duke	52	39	91

FG Pct: Maryland 65.5, Duke 58.6
FT Pct: Maryland 60.0, Duke 72.4
3FG Shooting: Maryland 5-11 (Williams 3-7, McLinton 1-1, Walsh 1-1, Downing 0-2); Duke 2-6 (Laettner 1-5, Davis 1-1).
Turnovers: Maryland 17, Duke 17
Blocks: Maryland 4, Duke 4 (Parks 2)
Steals: Maryland 4, Duke 3 (Laettner 2)
Fouled Out: Williams
Officials: Edsall, Higgins, Patillo
Attendance: 9,314

BOB DONNAN

ANITTA FRAZIER

> 99

We gave it away with no exe-
cution. It was a good effort
until the last four minutes. We
just weren't being tough and
this isn't a team that makes
excuses.
— *Thomas Hill*

February 23, 1992
Lawrence Joel Coliseum, Winston-Salem, NC

Duke	Min	FG M-A	FT M-A	Reb O-T	A	TP
Davis	26	4-8	4-5	0-1	1	12
Lang	30	1-2	4-4	4-6	0	6
Laettner	38	7-11	3-5	1-4	2	18
G. Hill	40	6-8	0-4	1-6	5	12
T. Hill	36	8-12	1-1	0-1	1	20
Parks	14	0-1	0-0	0-0	0	0
Clark	10	0-0	0-0	0-1	1	0
Blakeney	6	0-0	0-0	0-1	0	0
Totals	200	26-42	12-19	7-22	10	68

Wake Forest	Min	FG M-A	FT M-A	Reb O-T	A	TP
Rogers	34	9-11	0-1	1-6	2	18
King	26	3-7	3-4	0-0	3	9
Medlin	21	1-1	0-0	1-4	2	2
Tucker	39	9-15	6-10	1-2	0	24
McQueen	39	2-9	3-4	0-3	6	8
Hicks	10	1-1	0-0	1-2	0	2
Doggett	2	0-0	0-0	0-0	0	0
Rasmussen	3	0-0	2-2	0-0	0	2
Owens	26	3-4	1-1	4-4	3	7
Totals	200	28-48	15-22	8-21	16	72

Duke	35	33	68
Wake Forest	33	39	72

FG Pct: Duke 61.9, Wake Forest 58.3
FT Pct: Duke 63.2, Wake Forest 68.2
3FG Shooting: Duke 4-7 (T. Hill 3-4, Laettner 1-1, Davis 0-2); Wake Forest 1-6 (McQueen 1-6).
Turnovers: Duke 15, Wake Forest 12
Blocks: Duke 1 (T. Hill), Wake Forest 1
Steals: Duke 4 (Davis, T. Hill 2), Wake Forest 5
Fouled Out: Davis
Officials: Paparo, Hartzell, Croft
Attendance: 14,673 (stadium record)

duke vs. wake forest

The tightrope act the Blue Devils had been following finally broke at Wake Forest when Duke squandered a 10-point lead in the game's final five minutes in falling to the Deacons 72-68. Duke led 67-57 until what Coach K described as a "total breakdown" occurred. Missed free throws and unforced turnovers were much of the problem as Wake got hot. Derrick McQueen, 2-of-9 for the game, drilled a three-pointer to cut the lead to five and then Trelonnie Owens stripped the ball from **Christian Laettner** leading to another two points before making a three-point play to tie the score at 67. **Brian Davis** made 1-of-2 free throws and **Grant Hill** missed two more as Wake put the game away. An unsuccessful play (three-quar-ters length pass from Hill to Laettner) at the end of the game would later come back to make college basketball his-tory. With 11 of the top 12 teams in the country losing during the week, Duke stayed on top of the polls.

41

"

It was a great day for Christian. He showed what a big-time player he is. With Grant down and me not 100 percent, we needed Christian to have one of these games. He came through for us.
— *Bobby Hurley*

"

Christian made three-pointers and rebounded like crazy. He played with a passion; he played like a most valuable player.
— *Mike Krzyzewski*

BOB DONNAN

Talk about a roller coaster ride. First, Duke was coming off a loss to Wake Forest. Then, **Grant Hill** injured an ankle in practice the night before the Virginia game. Next, came the possible return of **Bobby Hurley** after a positive doctor's report the morning of Feb. 26. Almost forgotten was the anticipation of a future Duke legend getting his jersey retired. Finally, it all came together when **Christian Laettner** became the sixth player in Duke history to have his jersey hanging from the rafters in a pregame ceremony to set off a joyous night in Cameron Indoor Stadium. On cue, Laettner scored 32 points in the 76-67 defeat of the Cavaliers while Hurley gallantly returned to the fray with 26 minutes of action and nine assists. **Kenny Blakeney** got his first career start with Hill missing the contest and performed admirably. But this was Laettner's night as he also grabbed a season-high 13 rebounds, blocked a pair of shots and made 4-of-5 three-pointers with his family in attendance and an adoring crowd to cheer his every move.

BOB DONNAN

BOB DONNAN

February 26, 1992
Cameron Indoor Stadium, Durham, NC

Virginia	Min	FG M-A	FT M-A	Reb O-T	A	TP
Stith	39	8-20	0-0	3-5	3	17
Burrough	38	9-15	1-2	3-7	0	19
Jeffries	32	3-4	0-2	3-9	2	6
Oliver	24	4-9	0-0	0-4	0	8
Alexander	31	5-11	1-2	0-2	3	11
Parker	19	1-3	1-4	1-1	1	4
Barnes	8	0-1	0-0	0-0	0	0
Smith	9	1-1	0-0	0-0	3	2
Totals	200	31-64	3-10	11-31	12	67

Duke	Min	FG M-A	FT M-A	Reb O-T	A	TP
Davis	40	5-10	0-1	2-6	2	10
Lang	34	2-4	3-4	2-5	1	7
Laettner	31	12-21	4-5	2-13	1	32
Blakeney	15	3-4	0-2	0-0	2	6
T. Hill	36	4-8	2-2	2-4	3	11
Hurley	26	2-7	0-0	0-2	9	4
Meek	3	0-0	0-0	0-0	0	0
Clark	2	0-0	0-0	0-0	0	0
Parks	13	3-6	0-0	0-2	0	6
Totals	200	28-48	15-22	8-21	16	72

Virginia	32	35	67
Duke	34	42	76

FG Pct: Virginia 48.4, Duke 51.7
FT Pct: Virginia 30.0, Duke 64.3
3FG Shooting: Virginia 2-9 (Parker 1-2, Stith 1-3, Alexander 0-3, Oliver 0-1); Duke 5-13 (Laettner 4-5, T. Hill 1-2, Hurley 0-4, Davis 0-2).
Turnovers: Virginia 11, Duke 12
Blocks: Virginia 0, Duke 3 (Laettner 2)
Steals: Virginia 6, Duke 6 (Laettner, Blakeney 2)
Fouled Out: None
Officials: Wirtz, Scagliotta, Donato
Attendance: 9,314

BOB DONNAN

CHUCK LIDDY

Bobby Hurley might as well have said, "I'm Baaaack," while seniors **Christian Laettner** and **Brian Davis** showed that they had never left in Duke's exciting 75-65 victory over fourth-ranked UCLA. A national television audience looked on as Hurley canned back-to-back three-pointers in the second half of a tight contest and then engineered a 16-4 Duke run to end the game to give the Blue Devils their 23rd victory of the year. Laettner tallied 29 points and 13 rebounds, mostly against Don MacLean, and Davis added an inspired 19-point, 11-rebound performance. The Blue Devils scored a season-low 24 points in the first half as they adjusted to the presence of Hurley. Duke's fast break returned to form with Hurley back in command.

"

The little guy (Bobby Hurley) is really a courageous player. He was so stiff and sore but he came out and played 30 minutes and did a great job. He's a winner. He kept us together.
– *Mike Krzyzewski*

March 1, 1992
Pauley Pavilion, Los Angeles, CA

Duke	Min	FG M-A	FT M-A	Reb O-T	A	TP
Davis	34	6-11	7-10	0-11	4	19
Lang	32	2-3	1-6	5-9	1	5
Laettner	36	8-17	11-12	2-13	2	29
T. Hill	36	4-13	0-3	0-2	1	8
Hurley	36	3-5	3-4	0-0	4	11
Blakeney	13	1-1	0-0	0-3	0	3
Parks	11	0-0	0-0	1-1	0	0
Clark	1	0-0	0-0	0-0	0	0
Meek	1	0-0	0-0	0-0	0	0
Totals	200	24-50	22-35	8-41	12	75

UCLA	Min	FG M-A	FT M-A	Reb O-T	A	TP
MacLean	36	6-17	8-8	2-10	1	20
Murray	34	9-18	4-4	4-8	4	22
Butler	30	2-9	0-0	0-8	2	4
Madkins	31	4-7	0-0	1-2	4	8
Tarver	18	0-6	1-2	1-1	1	1
Zimmerman	4	0-1	0-0	0-0	0	0
Martin	15	0-3	3-3	1-1	1	3
O'Bannon	18	0-4	0-0	1-5	1	0
Edney	14	3-4	1-1	0-0	2	7
Totals	200	24-69	17-18	12-38	12	65

Duke	24	51	75
UCLA	29	36	65

FG Pct: Duke 48.0, UCLA 34.8
FT Pct: Duke 62.9, UCLA 94.4
3FG Shooting: Duke 5-12 (Laettner 2-4, Hurley 2-3, Blakeney, T. Hill 0-3, Davis 0-1); UCLA 0-14 (Murray 0-5, MacLean 0-2, Butler 0—2, Madkins 0-2, O'Bannon 0-2, Martin 0-1).
Turnovers: Duke 22, UCLA 15
Blocks: Duke 6 (T. Hill 4), UCLA 1
Steals: Duke 9 (Lang, Laettner 3), UCLA 11
Fouled Out: Butler
Officials: Range, Garibaldi, Harrington
Attendance: 13,023 (stadium record)

GENE WILBANKS

March 4, 1992 Littlejohn Coliseum, Clemson, SC

Duke	Min	FG M-A	FT M-A	Reb O-T	A	TP
Davis	35	9-15	11-12	1-6	2	30
Lang	31	3-6	8-8	4-7	1	14
Laettner	23	8-12	3-3	4-9	6	23
Hurley	34	2-9	5-6	0-2	8	11
T. Hill	24	3-10	3-3	2-6	0	11
Parks	11	1-3	0-0	1-4	0	2
Blakeney	16	0-2	0-0	0-0	0	0
Clark	9	0-1	0-0	0-0	3	0
Meek	13	3-4	1-3	2-3	1	7
Ast	4	0-1	0-0	0-0	1	0
Totals	200	29-63	31-35	16-39	21	98

Clemson	Min	FG M-A	FT M-A	Reb O-T	A	TP
Gray	20	6-10	0-0	0-2	1	13
Wallace	22	3-7	1-1	2-7	1	7
Hines	32	6-10	7-14	4-7	3	19
Whitney	32	5-11	2-2	1-1	10	17
Bovain	24	4-8	1-2	1-3	3	9
Wright	17	3-4	1-2	2-7	1	7
Harris	30	5-8	4-4	1-3	5	14
Burks	6	1-1	0-0	0-0	0	3
Amestoy	17	3-3	0-0	0-0	0	8
Totals	200	36-62	16-25	11-30	24	97

Duke	47	51	98
Clemson	52	45	97

FG Pct: Duke 46.0, Clemson 58.1
FT Pct: Duke 88.6, Clemson 64.0
3FG Shooting: Duke 9-22 (Laettner 4-4, Hurley 2-8, T. Hill 2-5, Davis 1-3, Blakeney 0-1, Ast 0-1); Clemson 9-18 (Whitney 5-10, Amestoy 2-2, Burks 1-1, Gray 1-1, Wallace 0-2, Bovain 0-2).
Turnovers: Duke 12, Clemson 10
Blocks: Duke 1 (Laettner), Clemson 0
Steals: Duke 6 (Lang, Davis, Blakeney 2), Clemson 4
Fouled Out: Lang, Whitney
Officials: Wirtz, Scagliotta, Corbin
Attendance: 11,500

VERN VERNA

It was predictable that Duke would have a UCLA hangover and its eyes set for the weekend matchup with North Carolina, but it was crazy to think that the top-ranked Blue Devils would be down by 15 points in the second half of their game against lowly Clemson. But it was true and Mike Krzyzewski couldn't stand it any longer when he sent five subs - **Christian Ast, Kenny Blakeney, Marty Clark, Erik Meek** and **Cherokee Parks** - into the game with 16:01 to play and the scoreboard reading, Clemson 66, Duke 51. Taking advantage of their opportunity, the Duke fivesome outscored the Tigers 8-2 after getting down by 19 points. Meek led the way with six straight points. Inspired, the starters returned five minutes later to settle the come-from-behind victory, 98-97. **Brian Davis** led all scorers with a career-high 30 points and **Christian Laettner** put Duke ahead to stay at 95-92 with a three-pointer.

"

We wanted to prove we could play good basketball. We huddled and said we were going to contribute. Everybody on this team wants to win.
– *Erik Meek*

45

RON FERRELL

46

It's hard to live up to the billing of a classic confrontation but this traditional season-ender between Duke and North Carolina was that, plus much more. The last home game for seniors **Christian Laettner**, **Brian Davis** and **Ron Burt** put the Cameron Crazies in a sentimental and celebrant mood. Laettner led the way with 26 points but was equaled by Tar Heel senior Hubert Davis who scored 35 points with six three-pointers. Those two heavy-weights put their respective teams in a tie at 71-71 with just under six minutes to play in the game which featured technicals on both Coach K and Dean Smith. Duke then put a crushing 18-6 run together to close out the game. All five Duke starters contributed in the run, including six points from **Thomas Hill** who finished the game with 18. **Grant Hill** returned to the fold after a two-week absence and **Bobby Hurley** was back at full strength with 19 points and five three-pointers. In the end, the Cameron crowd rushed the court and Laettner and Davis addressed their fellow students with "thank you's" for a great four-year run in which Duke piled up a 58-2 record at home, including this memorable 89-77 triumph over UNC.

"

I'm sure for those people who have watched ACC basketball for a number of years, it had to strike them as one of the great games in the history of the conference.
– Mike Krzyzewski

BOB DONNAN

March 8, 1992
Cameron Indoor Stadium, Durham, NC

North Carolina	Min	FG M-A	FT M-A	Reb O-T	A	TP
Reese	25	5-9	0-0	3-6	1	11
Lynch	32	5-8	0-0	4-6	5	10
Montross	24	4-6	1-2	1-2	0	9
Phelps	33	3-9	0-0	1-1	9	6
Davis	35	13-19	3-4	0-1	1	35
Sullivan	16	0-1	0-0	0-1	1	0
Salvadori	19	1-4	0-0	2-6	0	2
Rodl	13	1-4	2-2	1-2	1	4
Williams	2	0-2	0-0	0-1	1	0
Burgess	1	0-0	0-0	0-0	0	0
Totals	200	32-62	6-8	14-28	19	77

Duke	Min	FG M-A	FT M-A	Reb O-T	A	TP
Davis	37	3-8	2-2	3-5	4	8
Lang	28	5-6	0-0	3-5	1	10
Laettner	36	8-13	5-6	3-8	3	26
Hurley	36	7-15	0-0	1-2	7	19
T. Hill	36	7-15	3-4	2-4	1	18
G. Hill	21	3-5	2-2	1-4	3	8
Parks	5	0-0	0-0	0-0	0	0
Burt	1	0-1	0-0	0-0	0	0
Totals	200	33-63	12-14	14-30	19	89

North Carolina	46	31	77
Duke	46	43	89

FG Pct: North Carolina 51.6, Duke 52.4
FT Pct: North Carolina 75.0, Duke 85.7
3FG Shooting: UNC 7-12 (Davis 6-8, Reese 1-2, Rodl 0-1, Williams 0-1); Duke 11-24 (Laettner 5-8, Hurley 5-10, T. Hill 1-6).
Turnovers: North Carolina 14, Duke 9
Blocks: North Carolina 3, Duke 4 (Laettner 3)
Steals: North Carolina 5, Duke 4 (four players)
Fouled Out: None
Officials: Paparo, Rose, Edsall
Attendance: 9,314

OVERLEAF PHOTO BY BOB DONNAN

Duke recorded its third victory of the season over Maryland in its ACC Tournament opener at the Charlotte Coliseum. But for the third straight time it didn't come easy as the Terps hung tough in Duke's 94-87 victory. Even if it didn't appear pretty, the Blue Devils were getting back to full strength after several injuries in the final weeks of the season. **Bobby Hurley** was solid with 13 assists and just one turnover while scoring 16 points. **Christian Laettner** continued his torrid streak with 33 points while **Cherokee Parks** got involved with 11 minutes in his first ACC Tournament game.

It has to make you excited to know you can beat a team and not play your best. But we're getting close.
– *Bobby Hurley*

March 13, 1992
Charlotte Coliseum, Charlotte, NC
ACC Tournament Quarterfinals

Maryland	Min	FG M-A	FT M-A	Reb O-T	A	TP
Burns	35	9-15	7-11	6-10	1	25
Broadnax	38	2-6	8-8	1-6	5	12
Kerwin	27	1-5	0-1	3-7	0	2
McLinton	33	7-12	3-3	2-5	8	17
Williams	39	9-29	5-6	3-7	2	25
Walsh	17	2-5	0-0	3-9	1	4
Downing	6	0-0	2-2	0-1	0	2
Shultz	3	0-0	0-0	0-0	0	0
Bristol	2	0-0	0-0	0-0	0	0
Rainge	1	0-1	0-0	0-0	0	0
Horton	1	0-0	0-0	0-0	0	0
Totals	200	30-73	25-31	19-47	17	87

Duke	Min	FG M-A	FT M-A	Reb O-T	A	TP
Lang	18	3-6	2-4	1-1	2	8
Davis	35	7-12	3-4	4-6	1	17
Laettner	38	11-23	8-13	5-16	3	33
Hurley	38	4-10	6-6	0-2	13	16
T. Hill	34	5-15	2-3	2-3	1	12
G. Hill	22	1-5	3-6	2-4	0	5
Parks	11	1-3	1-2	2-5	0	3
Blakeney	2	0-0	0-0	1-1	0	0
Burt	1	0-0	0-0	0-0	0	0
Clark	1	0-0	0-0	0-0	0	0
Totals	200	32-74	25-38	20-48	20	94

Maryland	44	43	87
Duke	49	45	94

FG Pct: Maryland 41.1, Duke 43.2
FT Pct: Maryland 80.6, Duke 65.8
3FG Shooting: Maryland 2-9 (Williams 2-9); Duke 5-11 (Laettner 3-6, Hurley 2-3, Davis 0-1, T. Hill 0-1).
Turnovers: Maryland 13, Duke 10
Blocks: Maryland 3, Duke 7 (G. Hill 5)
Steals: Maryland 6, Duke 10 (Laettner 5)
Fouled Out: Burns, McLinton
Officials: Scagliotta, Rose, Rote
Attendance: 23,532

ALL ACC TOURNAMENT PHOTOS BY BOB DONNAN

Duke continued to pick up steam for its annual March run with a crushing 89-76 victory over Georgia Tech in the ACC semifinals. The Blue Devils began the game with a 23-6 lead and pushed it to 43-25 at the half to decide the outcome quickly in Charlotte. **Bobby Hurley** joined **Brian Davis** with a team-leading 17 points as the Duke defense stifled Tech early. Three Tech starters didn't hit a field goal in the first half and the whole team connected on just 10-of-30 shots. **Thomas Hill,** as always, was super on defense while **Marty Clark** was among the Duke reserves who totalled 52 minutes to give the starters an extra lift going into the ACC final.

"

We're pretty much back to the way we were playing. We were in the passing lanes; we were running. We were having fun.
— *Grant Hill*

March 14, 1992
Charlotte Coliseum, Charlotte, NC
ACC Tournament Semifinals

Georgia Tech

	Min	FG M-A	FT M-A	Reb O-T	A	TP
Mackey	40	11-13	3-7	6-7	0	25
Forrest	31	6-15	3-5	4-7	3	15
Geiger	18	2-5	0-0	2-4	2	4
Best	37	2-8	0-0	0-2	7	5
Barry	34	5-14	1-2	1-4	5	15
Newbill	15	1-1	0-0	1-2	1	2
B. Hill	16	3-7	0-0	0-0	1	7
Vinson	9	1-2	0-0	1-1	1	3
Totals	200	31-65	7-14	18-32	20	76

Duke

	Min	FG M-A	FT M-A	Reb O-T	A	TP
Lang	24	2-2	5-6	3-4	0	9
Davis	30	8-15	1-1	1-6	1	17
Laettner	29	4-6	6-7	2-5	5	15
Hurley	35	6-9	4-4	0-1	2	17
T. Hill	30	2-5	6-6	0-1	2	10
G. Hill	25	5-8	3-3	1-5	5	13
Parks	15	2-3	0-0	0-1	3	4
Blakeney	5	0-0	0-0	0-1	0	0
Meek	2	1-1	0-0	0-0	0	2
Clark	4	1-2	0-0	0-1	0	2
Ast	1	0-1	0-0	0-0	0	0
Totals	200	31-52	25-27	8-28	18	89

Georgia Tech	25	51	76
Duke	43	46	89

FG Pct: Tech 47.7, Duke 59.6
FT Pct: Tech 50.0, Duke 92.6
3FG Shooting: Tech 7-21 (Barry 4-11, Best 1-5, Hill 1-3, Vinson 1-2); Duke 2-6 (Laettner 1-2, Hurley 1-2, T. Hill 0-1, Davis 0-1).
Turnovers: Tech 14, Duke 12
Blocks: Tech 1, Duke 3 (Parks 2)
Steals: Tech 8, Duke 8 (Lang 4)
Fouled Out: Geiger
Officials: Hartzell, Edsall, Gordon
Attendance: 23,532

Brian Davis and **Christian Laettner** had won just about every prize imaginable in their four-year Duke careers except one, the ACC Championship. That trophy can now reside next to all others after the Blue Devils crushing 94-74 defeat of North Carolina in the 1992 ACC final. Laettner left nothing to chance with 25 points, 10 rebounds, seven steals and an awe-inspiring 5-of-8 shooting day from three-point range. But Laettner also had plenty of help with five others in double-figures, including **Grant Hill** who hit all eight of his shots and added seven assists. Bobby Hurley dished out a title game record 11 assists to make his three-game total 26 and his career total 50. All ACC records. Brian Davis was outstanding on defense, particularly against Hubert Davis who scored an inconsequential 19 points. It was a day of champions for the Blue Devils and a slight bit of redemption for the previous year's 22-point loss in the final to UNC.

March 15, 1992
Charlotte Coliseum, Charlotte, NC
ACC Tournament Championship

North Carolina	Min	FG M-A	FT M-A	Reb O-T	A	TP
Reese	26	4-10	1-1	2-3	4	9
Lynch	25	7-11	1-2	3-5	2	15
Montross	32	4-6	0-0	1-5	0	8
Phelps	34	4-8	0-0	1-3	10	9
Davis	34	8-12	1-2	1-1	2	19
Rodl	16	0-1	2-2	1-2	4	2
Sullivan	10	3-5	0-0	1-2	0	8
Wenstrom	3	0-2	0-0	0-0	0	0
Williams	4	0-2	0-0	0-0	2	0
Salvadori	8	2-2	0-0	0-0	0	4
Stephenson	2	0-0	0-0	0-0	0	0
Cherry	2	0-0	0-0	0-0	0	0
Burgess	2	0-0	0-0	0-0	0	0
Smith	2	0-1	0-0	0-0	0	0
Totals	200	32-60	5-7	14-26	24	74

Duke	Min	FG M-A	FT M-A	Reb O-T	A	TP
Lang	22	5-8	1-1	4-4	1	11
Davis	33	4-7	3-4	1-2	4	12
Laettner	38	8-12	4-5	4-10	0	25
Hurley	39	5-14	0-0	1-2	11	11
T. Hill	29	5-10	2-2	2-3	0	13
G. Hill	27	8-8	4-4	1-3	7	20
Parks	5	0-1	0-0	0-0	0	0
Blakeney	2	0-0	0-0	0-1	0	0
Ast	1	1-1	0-0	1-1	0	2
Meek	1	0-0	0-0	0-0	0	0
Clark	2	0-0	0-0	0-0	0	0
Burt	1	0-1	0-0	0-0	0	0
Totals	200	36-62	14-16	16-30	23	94

North Carolina	36	38	74
Duke	44	50	94

FG Pct: North Carolina 53.3, Duke 58.1
FT Pct: North Carolina 71.4, Duke 87.5
3FG Shooting: UNC 5-12 (Davis 2-3, Sullivan 2-4, Phelps 1-3, Reese 0-2, Williams 0-1); Duke 8-18 (Laettner 5-8, Hurley 1-5, T. Hill 1-3, Davis 1-2).
Turnovers: North Carolina 18, Duke 14
Blocks: North Carolina 2, Duke 5 (Parks, Laettner 2)
Steals: North Carolina 5, Duke 14 (Laettner 7)
Fouled Out: Lynch, Montross
Officials: Wirtz, Paparo, Scagliotta
Attendance: 23,532

"

I didn't think they could play better than they did against us in Durham last week, but they did. They were just remarkable.
– *Dean Smith*

"

It's tough to single out one guy. A lot of guys did a lot of dirty work. We played like champions. That's why we won.
– *Mike Krzyzewski*

BACK
TO BACK

The Story of Duke's 1992 NCAA Basketball Championship

The NCAA Tournament

By Mike Cragg

CHUCK LIDDY

THE NATION'S COLLECTIVE EYES ANNUALLY CAST upon the spring event known as the NCAA Tournament or "March Madness." In recent years the majority of the fans, media, coaches, and players' eyes have focused squarely on a basketball team representing Duke University. With eight straight trips to the NCAAs, Final Four berths every year but one since 1986, and the 1991 championship securely

under its belt, the 1992 Duke squad was looking to make history when it opened the tournament on March 19.

There seemed to be more at stake this year. It was a little different as the Blue Devils were now seen as the hunted, rather than in their familiar role as the hunter. The new label came from a record-breaking season of wire-to-wire number one rankings and a healthy 28-2 record, not to mention the presence of three All-Americas in the lineup and the winningest active coach in NCAA Tournament play, Mike Krzyzewski. In other words, all eyes were on Duke.

Duke was placed in the East Regional for the 12th time in school history and was paired

On the eve of the 1992 NCAA Tournament....

The only motivation we have year in and year out is doing the best with what we have. We think we're the best team in the country, not because we have the best talent but because we have the best coach and the best system. Our motivation to win (the NCAA Tournament) is because we think we should win and we can win.
– *Brian Davis*

I know I'm excited to play and ready to go. This is what the whole season was for. There is a sense of urgency. The whole season prepared us for this tournament. We have to put everything we won behind us and start over. We have to play six good basketball games.
– *Grant Hill*

There has been so much so-called pressure on this team all year long. We don't look like a team under pressure. We're excited about the opportunity to do something that's special, that's unique. I don't see why that should be pressure. What a fantastic opportunity for us.
– *Mike Krzyzewski*

CHUCK LIDDY

with Campbell University in a first round matchup in Greensboro, N.C. Duke earned the regional's number one seed after claiming the ACC regular season and tournament championships. Contrary to popular belief, it was the first time since 1986 that Duke was a number one seed.

Fortunately, some of the glare of the national spotlight spilled over to Duke's first round opponent from Buies Creek, N.C. People were enthralled with this small school, the unusual nickname (Camels), its quick-talking coach Billy Lee and their quest to knock off Goliath. The Duke players and coaches were happy to let the spotlight fall upon someone else.

Nonetheless, the scene at Duke's open practice session the night before the tournament was more reminiscent of a rock concert than a college basketball practice. Over 5,000 people, many screaming teenagers, filled the lower portions of the coliseum to get a glimpse of Christian Laettner and Bobby Hurley. After the one hour practice the team tried to board its bus but was stopped by a crowd that filled every space between the doors of the coliseum and the waiting vehicle. Police eventu-

ally escorted the team to a side door after being unable to persuade the crowd to make a path for the team. The practice hysteria around Duke was repeated on every stop of the NCAA Tournament but this was the only time the team wasn't able to board its own bus.

The games, however, were the important part of Duke's quest for a second straight national championship. Six games were all that stood between the Blue Devils and becoming the first repeat champions since UCLA's reign from 1967-73. In reality, Coach K only stressed two games at a time. Each weekend was seen as a new "tournament" until finally there were only four teams left with the same quest, to be the national champion.

In that first game, the Campbell players, with its tallest being 6'-6", played with nothing to lose and put their hearts out on the court. It was that kind of emotion and conviction that Coach K desired from his team as well. He got it. Of course, the talent and athleticism on the Duke side didn't hurt either. Duke's defense limited Campbell to just 16 points and 18.8 percent shooting from the field in the first half as the Blue Devils opened a 20-point halftime lead.

Laettner had 22 points and five steals in 32 minutes of action while guard Thomas Hill was fabulous in connecting on 8-of-10 shots for 20 points and grabbing five rebounds. Coach K cleared

58

March 19, 1992
Greensboro Coliseum, Greensboro, NC
NCAA Tournament First Round

Campbell	Min	FG M-A	FT M-A	Reb O-T	A	TP
Mocnik	36	11-23	0-0	2-10	0	29
Spinks	31	2-10	0-0	3-7	3	6
Ellison	33	0-6	2-4	5-5	2	2
Ison	35	3-12	1-2	2-3	4	7
Martin	29	4-12	0-0	0-1	4	10
Murray	1	0-0	0-0	0-1	0	0
Hall	8	0-1	2-2	0-1	0	2
Holley	1	0-0	0-0	0-0	0	0
Neely	16	0-5	0-0	3-5	0	0
Rice	3	0-1	0-0	0-0	0	0
Mitchell	7	0-1	0-0	1-1	0	0
Totals	200	20-71	5-8	22-43	13	56

Duke	Min	FG M-A	FT M-A	Reb O-T	A	TP
Lang	28	3-5	0-0	1-3	1	6
Davis	28	3-5	1-2	0-2	3	7
Laettner	32	9-14	2-3	1-9	4	22
Hurley	35	3-8	0-0	0-3	10	10
T. Hill	25	8-10	3-5	1-5	1	20
G. Hill	22	1-4	3-6	0-5	5	5
Parks	12	2-4	0-0	2-5	0	4
Clark	6	2-4	0-0	1-2	0	4
Meek	7	2-3	0-0	1-1	1	4
Blakeney	1	0-0	0-0	0-0	0	0
Burt	1	0-1	0-0	0-1	1	0
Ast	3	0-1	0-0	1-1	0	0
Totals	200	33-59	11-19	9-40	26	82

Campbell	16	40	56
Duke	36	46	82

FG Pct: Campbell 28.2, Duke 55.9
FT Pct: Campbell 62.5, Duke 57.9
3FG Shooting: Campbell 11-27 (Mocnik 7-13, Spinks 2-4, Martin 2-7, Neely 0-3); Duke 5-12 (Hurley 2-4, Laettner 2-3, T. Hill 1-2, Davis 0-1, Clark 0-1, G. Hill 0-1).
Turnovers: Campbell 21, Duke 16
Blocks: Campbell 0, Duke 8 (Lang, G. Hill 2)
Steals: Campbell 8, Duke 13 (Laettner 5)
Fouled Out: Spinks, Mitchell, Ison
Officials: Bair, Bova, Askew
Attendance: 15,800

CHUCK LIDDY

Duke-Campbell....

The key thing for us is to play hard and play good defense. It was a matter of me getting into a defensive mode. That helps me get into my offense. I was really up for playing and my shots were falling.
– Thomas Hill

It was a good game for us. Both teams played hard. They put us in a position that we had to play hard. Otherwise, it might have been a much closer game.
– Mike Krzyzewski

CHUCK LIDDY

the bench in the game's waning moments as Marty Clark, Cherokee Parks and Erik Meek each scored four points. Krzyzewski knew he needed each of their contributions in the weeks ahead which made the 82-56 Duke victory a good starting point.

It was ironic that Duke's second round opponent in the 1992 NCAA Tournament was also its second round opponent in the 1991 NCAA Tournament. The Iowa Hawkeyes returned all five starters who suffered through the previous year's surprisingly easy 85-70 Duke win in Minneapolis. Tops among them was center Acie Earl who had become friends with Brian Davis after the two were on a summer all-star tour of Europe. Earl and his teammates had hoped for and now had gotten a return matchup with the Blue Devils.

Like the year before, Duke got out to a tremendous start with its stifling defense. This time a partisan Greensboro Coliseum crowd of 15,800 urged on every Duke move. Iowa shot just 29 percent from the field in the first half and 38.7 for the game while the Blue Devils opened an insurmountable 24-point halftime cushion at 48-24. Toss in the 13 turnovers Duke forced in the first frame and you can understand the reason Duke students chanted jokingly, "Camels better!" Iowa hung tough with a 2-3 zone and multiple presses to make the final score, 75-62, respectable.

Earl did his best with 19 points, 12 rebounds and eight blocked shots but Laettner was equal to the task with 19 points and eight rebounds. Brian Davis led five Duke scorers in double-figures with 21 points to go with his 10 rebounds. The Blue Devils shot poorly but it hardly mattered as Iowa was only able to cut the Duke lead to eight in the second half. Duke scored 17 second-chance

> "

Duke-Iowa....

The first eight minutes of the game were great, just pure fun. We knew Iowa wanted very badly to come in and beat us. It was very intense and we were playing very good defense.
– Christian Laettner

We can't have lapses. I think we did a great job coming back after that lapse in the second half. It is hard because sometimes mentally you can get out of the game when you have such a big lead.
– Antonio Lang

We realize we were defeated by an outstanding team. Duke does so many things and has so many dimensions that they're very, very tough to defend.
– Tom Davis
Iowa coach

CHUCK LIDDY

Duke-Seton Hall....

When my brother was out there, it was a weird situation. It was real distracting. It was the hardest thing I had to do this year. My whole game is concentration and intensity. Running the team was hard for me with my concentration and intensity not up to the level where it usually is.
– *Bobby Hurley*

CHUCK LIDDY

points in the first half and limited Iowa to only four. In all, Duke had 22 offensive rebounds and grabbed a 46 to 33 advantage in the rebound category.

It was on to Philadelphia and the "City of Brotherly Love" was the stage for the battle of Hurley brothers in the regional semifinal matchup between

Duke and Seton Hall. Duke's Bobby (a junior) and Seton Hall's Danny (a freshman) were the subject of most of the pregame conversation, including their parents on ABC's "Good Morning America" the day of the game. Both had played for their father, Bob Sr., at St. Anthony High School in Jersey City but had never played in a game against each other, so it was no surprise that the normal pregame butterflies grew a little larger this time. The game also featured a coaching matchup of close friends P.J. Carlesimo and Krzyzewski.

The two teams flexed their defensive muscles early and often to turn the game into a halfcourt battle of attrition. For every Seton Hall move, Duke had a countermove and in the end Duke found an unlimited supply of timely offense, both inside and outside, to win 81-69 in The Spectrum. Duke led only 48-44 with 15 minutes left in the game, then delivered the knockout punch with a 16-

"

Both teams played outstanding defense. I thought Tony (Lang) gave us a big, big lift, in the first half especially. Thomas scored well but his defense on Karnishovas or Leahy and sometimes on Dehere was a key factor in the ballgame. This was one of the toughest games we've played all season.
— *Mike Krzyzewski*

Seton Hall did a good job on us defensively, but we had a lot of guys who stepped up. The whole game, they played very good defense on me, and the thing they did best of all was not to let the pass get to me.
— *Christian Laettner*

CHUCK LIDDY

Duke-Kentucky....

All I kept thinking (at the end of the Duke-Kentucky game) was I didn't want to be watching the Final Four on television. I didn't want to miss out on my third Final Four in three years. I didn't want to lose.
– Bobby Hurley

They call this lunacy, this NCAA Tournament, March Madness. But never, ever, has it been madder, and grander, than this.
– Bill Lyon
Philadelphia Inquirer

The game ends. The story never will. The dream wilts. The legacy blossoms. The moment fades. The memories multiply. Ship the videotape to the Basketball Hall of Fame via express mail. This is the game's centennial season. We may dribble 100 years more before we see another game that fills an arena with more energy.
– Rick Bozich
Louisville Courier-Journal

CHUCK LIDDY

7 burst to go up 64-51.

Laettner led the way with 16 points and knocked in a fall-away jumper after Seton Hall had closed to within 68-62. He then rebounded a Danny Hurley miss with 2:45 left to seal the outcome and turn the game into a free throw shooting contest. The Blue Devils won that contest easily hitting 24-of-31 free throws while the Pirates were just 8-of-14. Sophomore Antonio Lang matched Laettner with 16 points and hauled down seven rebounds while the Hills - Thomas and Grant - had 13 apiece. Thomas was also spectacular on the defensive side.

As for the Hurleys, it was a game they would probably rather forget. Bobby had seven assists, but six turnovers limited his normal sure-handed leadership while Danny played a season-high 18 minutes but was 0-of-4 from the field. The good thing was Bobby had more games to look forward to.

The NCAA Tournament had now boiled down to just eight teams fighting for the right to play in Minneapolis and the 1992 Final Four. It was familiar territory for the Blue Devils. Every member of the team, except for the freshman and walk-on Ron Burt, had been to the Final Four every season of their collegiate career. They knew no other conclusion to their season. In 1989, Christian Laettner, then a freshman, outdueled Alonzo Mourning with 24 points on 9-of-10 shooting from the field and the Blue Devils knocked off top-seeded Georgetown 85-77. In 1990, Laettner pro-

pelled the team past top-seeded Connecticut with a miraculous lean-in jumper with 1.6 seconds to play in overtime for a 79-78 victory. And in 1991, Duke simply dominated St. John's behind Hurley's 20 points and Laettner's 19 points for a 78-61 win in the Midwest Regional Final.

Could Duke do it again? Did Christian Laettner have another miracle in his pocket? Or would Duke even need a miracle? The answers - yes, Yes, and YES!

Just hearing the schools Duke and Kentucky together is something special for college basketball historians. Two of the most famed programs in history were about to take aim at each other again. The two had met before with greater stakes in other eras. The 1966 national semifinal had Kentucky pull out an 83-79 win despite the 29 points from Duke's Jack Marin, and in 1978 the NCAA championship came down to the two schools. That game featured the favored Wildcats against the giant-killers from Duke under the direction of Bill Foster. Kentucky also came out on top in that one by a heartbreaking 94-88 count. The Duke group did get some measure of revenge in 1980 when the Blue Devils beat Kentucky 55-54 on its homecourt in the Mideast Regional semifinals.

This was 1992, however, and now it was Krzyzewski and Rick Pitino; Laettner and Jamal Mashburn; Hurley and Sean Woods; all names that will live in tourna-

CHUCK LIDDY

March 28, 1992
The Spectrum, Philadelphia, PA
NCAA East Regional Final

Kentucky	Min	FG M-A	FT M-A	Reb O-T	A	TP
Mashburn	43	11-16	3-3	5-10	3	28
Pelphrey	25	5-7	3-3	0-1	5	16
Martinez	23	2-4	0-0	0-0	1	5
Woods	38	9-15	2-2	1-2	9	21
Farmer	15	2-3	4-6	0-1	1	9
Feldhaus	37	2-6	1-2	1-1	5	5
Brown	30	6-11	3-5	1-3	0	18
Ford	7	0-2	0-0	1-1	0	0
Timberlake	5	0-0	1-2	0-0	0	1
Riddick	1	0-0	0-0	0-0	0	0
Braddy	1	0-1	0-0	0-0	0	0
Totals	200	37-65	12-22	10-21	24	103

Duke	Min	FG M-A	FT M-A	Reb O-T	A	TP
Lang	21	2-2	0-1	2-3	0	4
Davis	38	3-6	7-10	2-5	1	13
Laettner	43	10-10	10-10	1-7	3	31
Hurley	45	6-12	5-6	0-3	10	22
T. Hill	34	6-10	5-5	0-3	2	19
G. Hill	37	5-10	1-2	6-10	7	11
Parks	6	2-2	0-0	0-0	0	4
Clark	1	0-0	0-0	0-0	0	0
Totals	200	34-52	28-34	11-31	23	104

Kentucky	45	48	10	103
Duke	50	43	11	104

FG Pct: Kentucky 56.9, Duke 65.4
FT Pct: Kentucky 73.9, Duke 82.4
3FG Shooting: Kentucky 12-22 (Mashburn 3-4, Pelphrey 3-4, Brown 3-5, Martinez 1-2, Farmer 1-2, Woods 1-1, Feldhaus 0-2, Ford 0-1, Braddy 0-1); Duke 8-16 (Hurley 5-10, T. Hill 2-3, Laettner 1-1, Davis 0-2).
Turnovers: Kentucky 12, Duke 20.
Blocks: Kentucky 0, Duke 3 (G. Hill, Parks, Clark)
Steals: Kentucky 12, Duke 8 (T. Hill 3)
Fouled Out: Mashburn, Martinez, Davis
Officials: Higgins, Range, Clark
Attendance: 17,878

There have been noted upsets. There have been countless games played at a high level, and for great stakes. But no other college game has ever combined, in one package, this much meaning, this much expertise and this much drama. Duke-Kentucky was the greatest college game of them all.
– Bob Ryan
Boston Globe

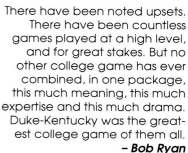

OVERLEAF PHOTO BY CHUCK LIDDY
Copyright Durham Herald Co., Inc, 1992

ment history after the game of March 28.

Kentucky did everything possible to dethrone the champions and appeared to have Duke right where it wanted them with 2.1 seconds to play in the overtime period after Sean Woods drove by Hurley and banked in a one-handed shot over Laettner for a one-point lead. Kentuckians were celebrating from one corner of the state to the other with a narrow 103-102 lead.

In Duke's most desperate hour, Hurley called an immediate timeout and Krzyzewski huddled his team to map out an attack. Everything would have to work to perfection and Coach K showed his confidence by suddenly stating, "We're going to win this game and here is how we're going to do it." Even he had *some* doubts but the players needed to feel confident when they stepped on the court for the final seconds.

Then, in a season equally filled with magical moments and overwhelming adversity, a miracle took place.

Grant Hill flung the undefended inbounds pass to Laettner who leaped to catch the ball over John Pelphrey and Deron Feldhaus. Time seemed to stand still as Laettner faked to his right, turned to his left and lofted an 18-footer that found nothing but net as time expired. With its collective breath held for the two seconds, the Spectrum crowd erupted as the Duke players jumped on Laettner to celebrate another trip to the Final Four and a 104-103 victory over Kentucky.

But really that was just the exclamation point on a terrific basketball game. Laettner was simply perfect. He hit all 10 of his field goal attempts and all 10 of his free throws to finish the game with 31 points and set new tournament records for shooting accuracy. Laettner also

OFFICIAL TIME

It was only two seconds, but it seemed
longer. After I caught the ball, I just
tried to create some distance, just
shoot the ball well.
– *Christian Laettner*

I never thought anything would ever top the excitement of the Connecticut shot. But this shot definitely did. There was no time to think (against Connecticut) - it just went boom-boom-boom. But I had a little more time to think about this shot. It was only two seconds, but it seemed longer. After I caught the ball, I just tried to create some distance, just shoot the ball well. I just thank God for giving me the opportunity to be a part of two such incredible games.
– Christian Laettner

When the pass was in the air, it felt like it took forever for it to come down. It was like watching a slow-motion movie sequence, like they had in "The Natural." It was weird. But as soon as Christian caught it, I felt confident. I've never seen one player make as many great plays as him.
– Grant Hill

We just call Christian "Always." That's his nickname, and he lived up to it again. He's always the man; he always comes through. Even when things look impossible, Christian always delivers.
– Brian Davis

I told my team, "We're going to win." In that situation, even if you're not sure you're going to win, you have to show confidence in the expression on your face and the words coming out of your mouth. I just thank God that I was able to be a part of one of the greatest games ever played. For a guy that loves basketball, you hope someday to be a part of something like this. You can't say enough, you can't write enough about how many great plays there were.
– Mike Krzyzewski

CHUCK LIDDY

became the NCAA Tournament's all-time scoring leader, passing Elvin Hayes' record of 358.

Duke led by five points at the half, 50-45, and upped the lead to 12 points before Kentucky's full-court press began to bother the Blue Devils. The Wildcats had several steals and big three-pointers to eventually tie the game at 81. Duke fell behind 89-87 then Brian Davis hit a jumper, Laettner tallied two free throws, and Thomas Hill hit the game-tying bucket with 1:03 left in regulation on a leaning jumper.

In overtime, John Pelphrey hit a three and Hurley responded with the same. Later, Laettner hit an incredible fade-away around two defenders with shot clock running out to put Duke ahead 100-98. Then it was Mashburn's turn as he hit a layup and was fouled to put Kentucky back ahead 101-100 with 19.6 seconds to play. Laettner then drew a foul and canned two free throws for a 102-101 lead with 7.8 seconds to play. Kentucky called time and set up Woods' one-handed drive but that was only a prelude to the final 2.1 seconds.

Some may begin to wonder if it is Duke's annual destiny to land in the Final Four. T-shirts even sprang up the final week of the season renaming the Final Four to "Duke and The Final Three". Coach K joined John Wooden as the only coach to take a team to five straight Final Fours with the Kentucky win and now had his team gearing up to duplicate another Wooden feat - back to back championships.

Up next was Indiana, an intriguing matchup between the two winningest programs in NCAA Tournament history. The media also focused on the battle of wits between Bob Knight and Krzyzewski,

who had played for Knight at Army and later coached with him at Indiana. Like politics, all of the extraneous focus had nothing to do with the final results.

For the second straight year, Bobby Hurley came to play at the Final Four. Against the Hoosiers he almost single-handedly kept Duke from getting blown out in the first half. Duke trailed by as many as 12 points, 39-27, in the first frame as Indiana shot 58.6 percent from field and dominated nearly every aspect of the game.

With 2:02 to play in the first half and down by 12, Hurley cut into the lead with a long three-pointer followed by two free throws. Thomas Hill joined in with a bank shot at 1:34 and a leaning jumper with 18.9 seconds to play. Hill was also fouled by Damon Bailey for the three-point play and Duke trailed by just five at the half, 42-37.

Everyone in the Metrodome knew that Duke was fortunate to be just five points down. The beginning of the second half turned into one of Duke's finest moments of the season. Coach K stressed defense at the half and defense is what he got. The Blue Devils reeled off 13 straight points and then made it a 21-3 surge to open the first 10 minutes of the frame to make the score 58-45 in favor of Duke. Wrapped in the middle was a technical foul on Knight, the ever-present Hurley and a ferocious, attacking defense which swarmed the Hoosiers at every turn.

In the fray, senior forward Brian Davis injured his ankle diving for a loose ball but that was the only down side of the first 10 minutes of the second frame. Davis' injury was costly as he would later miss the only start of his senior season in the next game against Michigan.

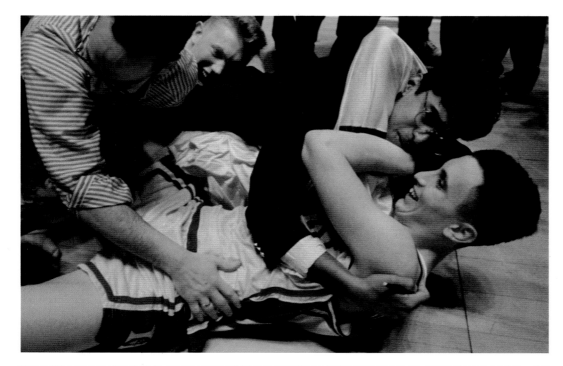

Gosh, wasn't that some ending of the Duke game?
– President George Bush
the day after the game

That's the greatest college basketball game ever. Pure, gut-stirring theater. Incredible doesn't do it justice."
– David Teel
Newport News Daily Press

Writers and broadcasters were left standing at their seats or just sitting. Glances were exchanged. Few words were spoken. A lot of heads just shook back and forth, back and forth. When Christian Laettner let fly the 17-foot missile that beat Kentucky on the last play of overtime, veteran writers who had seen hundreds of games knew they had witnessed something special. Perhaps something to retire on.
– Gary McCann
Greensboro News & Record

This wasn't just a game to get into the Final Four, it was an evening with fantasy. The longer it lasted, the more awesome it became. Whatever the 10 greatest college basketball games are, Duke-Kentucky 1992 has to be one of them.
– Frank Dascenzo
Durham Herald-Sun

Kentuckians learned Saturday night what North Carolinians have known for two years - that Duke, Laettner and Krzyzewski are the ultimate athletic warriors. The Blue Devils have given North Carolina and the ACC a definition of greatness unknown since '74, when State and Thompson established a grading scale that most believed would be impossible to match. Duke and Laettner have now matched it.
– Caulton Tudor
Raleigh News & Observer

BOB DONNAN

Duke led 69-61 with under two minutes to play when the outcome of the game came down to a duel between Duke's Marty Clark and Indiana's Todd Leary. Clark, in the game because of Davis' left ankle sprain, was the designated Indiana foulee, while the sophomore Leary, a player not even mentioned in Duke's pregame scouting report, was called on for long range bombing. It turned into a pretty impressive contest.

After the Hoosiers cut the lead to five, Clark made the first of five free throws in six attempts. Repeatedly, Indiana fouled while Leary drilled three straight three-pointers to pull within three at 78-75. A game seemingly won going away, turned interesting when Hurley stepped out of bounds on a Laettner throw-in. That gave Leary one more shot as CBS announcer Jim Nantz proclaimed, "The movie 'Hoosiers' is coming to life." Unlike the movie, Thomas Hill put the defensive clamp on Leary, denying him a chance at folklore status, and made him pass to Jamal Meeks who missed from the corner in front of the Indiana bench.

Free throws by Antonio Lang and Cherokee Parks closed out the 81-78 victory as the Blue Devils headed to the NCAA championship game for the third consecutive season. Hurley finished the day with a career-high six three-pointers and 26 points on a day when Laettner wasn't his normal self on offense (eight points). Grant Hill had 14 points off the bench on 6-of-9 shooting while Thomas Hill added 11 points.

The Fab Five meets The Victory Tour.

It sounds more like a rock concert promotion than a college basketball game but that's the billing Michigan and Duke had entering the Metrodome on April 6th to decide the national champion. Michigan's five freshman starters had surprised everyone in advancing to the title game after knocking off top-seeded Ohio State in the Southeast Regional Final and cinderella Cincinnati in Minneapolis. Ironically, the two teams had already met once in a December matchup in Ann Arbor when Duke prevailed by the narrowest of margins, 88-85, in overtime.

Grant Hill made his first start since February when he was inserted for an injured Brian Davis. Hill made the most of the opportunity in scoring 18 points and grabbing 10 rebounds as Duke stumbled out of the blocks but hung tough in trailing by just one at the half, 31-30. Having the most frustrating time of it was Laettner, the national player of the year, who had more turnovers (seven) than points (five) in the first half. But as champions prove time and again, he came back with a vengeance in the second frame, scoring 14 points and committing no turnovers.

It was the 20-minute second period which everyone on the Duke side remembers and put the Blue Devils back on the podium for a second straight season. Much like the Indiana contest, the Blue Devils turned up the defensive pressure and forced Michigan into 29 percent shooting from the field and just 20 second-half points. The scoreboard read 48-45 Duke with just 6:51 to play when the Blue Devils turned on the after-burners.

From that point, Duke outscored Michigan 23-6 as Laettner began the run with a twisting layup and a steal which led to a Grant Hill drive. Duke would not be denied in scoring on its final 12 possessions and clamping down on the Wolverines. Thomas Hill contributed with 16 points and seven rebounds, including a memorable offensive rebound and follow during the run.

With 13.5 seconds remaining and a comfortable 20-point cushion, Coach K gave his starters one last curtain call to an incredible season-long journey. Off the court came Antonio Lang, Bobby Hurley, Grant Hill, Christian Laettner and Thomas Hill. The injured Davis, who played a key 10 minutes in relief, was as demonstrative as anyone with his unabashed joy. A roar echoed through the dome as players exchanged high-fives and hugs to start the celebration of the 71-51 victory. The chants of "repeat" and "we're number one, twice" filled the players' ears for the next 30 minutes as the nets came down and Duke set itself apart from the college basketball world in claiming a perfect "Back To Back."

CHUCK LIDDY

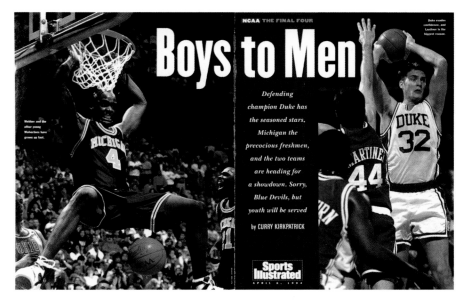

"

Duke-Indiana....

Bobby's play in the first half kept us in the game, so we would have a chance. In the first half we didn't have that emotion that we needed to play with.
– Mike Krzyzewski

I'm really proud of my teammates who don't play that much (Marty Clark and Cherokee Parks). They stepped up when we needed them. It's not our birthright to be here at the Final Four. Teams are not going to roll over and die.
– Grant Hill

I just wanted to get my rhythm. They were just free throws. You just have to make it, then make the next one. I expected to get fouled.
– Marty Clark
made five straight free throws in final two minutes

April 4, 1992
The Metrodome, Minneapolis, MN
NCAA National Semifinal

Indiana	Min	FG M-A	FT M-A	Reb O-T	A	TP
Cheaney	28	4-13	2-4	2-7	1	11
Henderson	32	6-9	2-2	2-5	1	15
Nover	20	3-4	2-2	2-3	0	9
Bailey	22	4-8	0-0	1-3	0	9
Reynolds	25	1-4	0-0	0-4	4	2
Meeks	18	1-2	1-2	1-3	8	3
Anderson	26	1-6	0-1	2-4	1	2
Graham	28	6-9	5-5	0-7	0	18
Leary	1	3-3	0-0	0-0	0	9
Totals	200	29-58	12-16	12-41	15	78

Duke	Min	FG M-A	FT M-A	Reb O-T	A	TP
Lang	27	1-5	2-2	1-3	0	4
Davis	25	1-3	3-7	3-5	0	5
Laettner	39	2-8	4-7	1-10	1	8
T. Hill	32	3-10	4-5	1-2	0	11
Hurley	37	7-12	6-8	0-0	4	26
G. Hill	29	6-9	2-4	3-6	6	14
Parks	9	3-5	2-3	1-1	0	8
Clark	2	0-0	5-76	0-1	0	5
Totals	200	23-52	28-42	10-30	11	81

Indiana	42	36	78
Duke	37	44	81

FG Pct: Indiana 50.0, Duke 44.2
FT Pct: Indiana 75.0, Duke 66.7
3FG Shooting: Indiana 8-15 (Leary 3-3, Cheaney 1-3, Graham 1-3, Henderson 1-1, Nover 1-1, Bailey 1-1, Meeks 0-1, Anderson 0-2); Duke 7-11 (Hurley 6-9, T. Hill 1-1, Laettner 0-1).
Turnovers: Indiana 17, Duke 12
Blocks: Indiana 3, Duke 6 (G. Hill 3)
Steals: Indiana 6, Duke 5 (T. Hill, Hurley 2)
Fouled Out: Cheaney, Henderson, Bailey, Graham, G. Hill
Officials: Higgins, Valentine, Clougherty
Attendance: 50,379

BOB DONNAN

74

"

Duke-Michigan....

It wasn't the prettiest game but we were resilient out there. We got the job done.
– Bobby Hurley

CHUCK LIDDY

April 6, 1992
The Metrodome, Minneapolis, MN
National Championship

Michigan	Min	FG M-A	FT M-A	Reb O-T	A	TP
Webber	29	6-12	2-5	4-11	1	14
Jackson	16	0-1	0-0	1-1	2	0
Howard	29	4-9	1-3	1-3	0	9
Rose	37	5-12	1-2	2-5	4	11
King	39	3-10	0-0	1-2	1	7
Riley	19	2-6	0-0	2-4	1	4
Voskuil	15	1-2	2-2	0-3	3	4
Pelinka	10	1-2	0-0	1-2	1	2
Hunter	2	0-0	0-0	0-0	0	0
Talley	1	0-2	0-0	1-1	0	0
Bossard	1	0-1	0-0	0-0	0	0
Seter	1	0-1	0-0	1-1	0	0
Armer	1	0-0	0-0	0-0	0	0
Totals	200	22-58	6-12	15-35	13	51

Duke	Min	FG M-A	FT M-A	Reb O-T	A	TP
Lang	31	2-3	1-2	2-4	0	5
G. Hill	36	8-14	2-2	5-10	5	18
Laettner	35	6-13	5-6	1-7	0	19
Hurley	36	3-12	2-2	0-3	7	9
T. Hill	34	5-10	5-8	3-7	0	16
Parks	13	1-3	2-2	2-3	0	4
Davis	10	0-2	0-0	0-0	0	0
Ast	1	0-0	0-0	0-1	0	0
Clark	1	0-0	0-0	0-0	0	0
Blakeney	1	0-0	0-0	0-0	0	0
Burt	1	0-0	0-0	0-0	0	0
Meek	1	0-0	0-0	0-0	0	0
Totals	200	25-57	17-22	14-37	12	71

Michigan	31	20	51
Duke	30	41	71

FG Pct: Michigan 37.9, Duke 43.9
FT Pct: Michigan 50.0, Duke 77.3
3FG Shooting: Michigan 1-11 (King 1-2, Rose 0-3, Webber 0-2, Howard 0-1, Voskuil 0-1, Talley 0-1, Bossard 0-1, Rose 0-3); Duke 4-9 (Laettner 2-4, Hurley 1-3, T. Hill 1-2).
Turnovers: Michigan 20, Duke 14
Blocks: Michigan 3, Duke 4 (G. Hill 2)
Steals: Michigan 8, Duke 9 (G. Hill 3)
Fouled Out: None
Officials: Donaghy, Harrington, Libbey
Attendance: 50,379

Coach was pretty upset at half-time. We simply weren't playing hard. We should know that, that playing hard is what it takes to win. In the second half, all the guys just stepped up. We started playing Duke defense. That was the difference.
– Thomas Hill

I think Michigan had a lot to do with our poor play. In the second half, we came out and did a better job. The most important thing is we got the second national title. It's the best feeling to go out in your last game at Duke as national champions.
– Christian Laettner

Grant's penetration was the key to the ballgame. He had patience on offense and created some things. One of their defenders had to come off Christian and Laettner can't be stopped - at least in the college game - when he's able to go one-on-one.
– Mike Krzyzewski

CHUCK LIDDY

CHUCK LIDDY

CHUCK LIDDY

CHUCK LIDDY

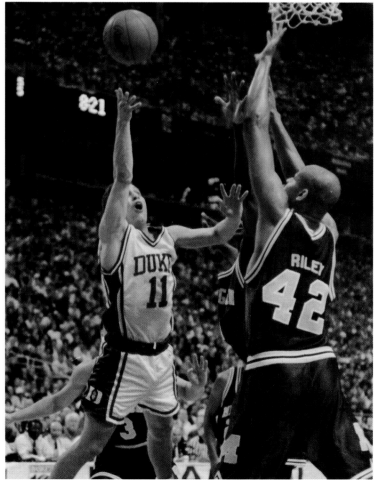
BRIAN SPURLOCK

"

No matter how good we are individually, we'd never be good if we weren't together.
– *Brian Davis*

This is the greatest year I've ever had coaching. It has been incredible coaching these guys. To be ranked number one all year, to do all the things they did, they deserve this. To beat out-standing teams like Michigan, Indiana, Seton Hall and Kentucky these last four games make it feel even better, like we really deserve it.
– *Mike Krzyzewski*

In this day and age, nobody but the guys on our team can say they've won two national championships. It's been such a long year, but all the work was worth it.
– *Thomas Hill*

It's something I'll think about when I get old and gray.
– *Antonio Lang*

CHUCK LIDDY

CHUCK LIDDY

This is what 100 years of basketball evolution has produced: Duke - The Perfect Program. Tommy Amaker to Hurley. Danny Ferry to Laettner to Parks. The Perfect Program continues on.
– Steve Wieberg
USA Today

They're a most deserving champion. They're one of the finest college basketball teams I've seen in a long time.
– Bill Walton

What Mike has done, given the way the tournament has changed, must compare favorably with what John Wooden did at UCLA. You just can't do what they have done. Yet they have done it. It is an incredible achievement.
– Steve Fisher
Michigan coach

The Sporting News

APRIL 13, 1992 / $2.50 ($2.95 Can.)

Do the A's still have it?

Whether Oakland can continue to dominate could be answered early

Plan B turns into exhibit A

Spending frenzy is evidence free agency could fell the NFL salary structure

NHL deadline could be taxing

The owners and players have until April 15 to save the season

IT'S DUKE

IT'S DUKE

Winning start
Knoblauch, Puckett help Twins beat Brewers 4-2 in the season opener

A perfect time
Kids tell Minnesotans how they'd design a day of their own

MINNEAPOLIS EDITION

StarTribune
NEWSPAPER OF THE TWIN CITIES

Minnesotans vote for their favorites today, but eyes are on N.Y.

'92 CAMPAIGN

Peru leader, army seize government

'Duke II,' the sequel
Laettner leads Devils' second-half surge

1992 Final Four
TWIN CITIES

2 arrested in death of elderly woman

Isaac Asimov, the master of science fiction, dies at age 72

High court tightens 'sting' rules in pornography case

Almanac

Today's weather:

DURHAM EDITION

BUSINESS CAT TUESDAY LOCAL/STATE WEATHER
IGNORED | PUNCTUAL PICKING | 'GROSSLY
ULTIMATUM | | MISLEADING'

The News & Observer
Raleigh, N.C.

Double Duke!

Two-timing Blue Devils take special place in game

Duke heat wilts Michigan, 71-51

'Pure ecstasy' for Cameron Crazies

Violent crash claims lives of 3 Russians

President suspends Peru's constitution

U.S. aid cut after a 'classic coup'

VETERANS HIGHLIGHT OPENERS

FASHION'S FLASHBACK

USA TODAY

NO. 1 IN THE USA · 6.6 MILLION READERS A DAY

NEWSLINE

N.Y. vote today's big prize

DUKE REPEATS TITLE

Shakes off Mich. 71-51

Primary critical for Clinton

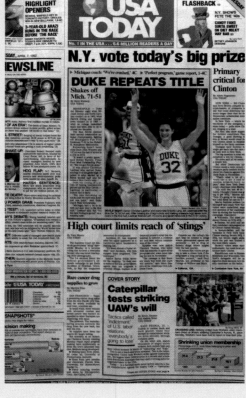

High court limits reach of 'stings'

COVER STORY
Caterpillar tests striking UAW's will

Shrinking union membership

ROCKET ON BULB: The NHL playoffs remain doubtful as strike continues / B5

SPORTS

B

LOCAL
BUSINESS
CLASSIFIEDS

No. 1: Coast-to-coast

Devils repeat championship

Laettner stepped forward

SOUVENIR EDITION

Blue Devils saved their best for last

Here's the pitch . . .
Bush's bouncer gets baseball off and running

PLAY BALL

APRIL 13, 1992 $2.95

Sports Illustrated

Dynasty

Duke, led by Bobby Hurley,
blitzes Michigan to become the
first repeat NCAA champion in 19 years

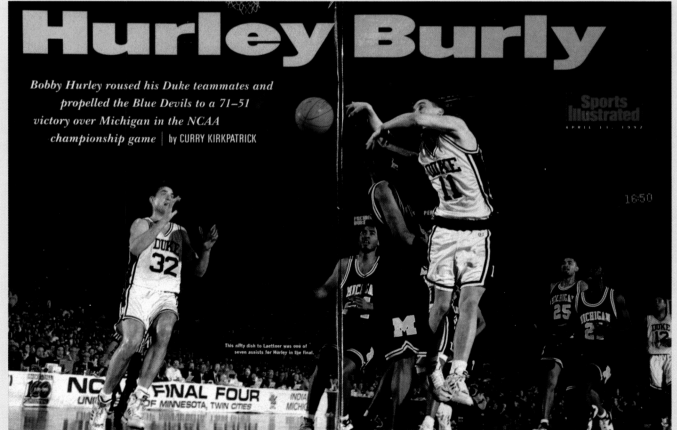

Hurley Burly

*Bobby Hurley roused his Duke teammates and
propelled the Blue Devils to a 71–51
victory over Michigan in the NCAA
championship game* | by CURRY KIRKPATRICK

Sports Illustrated
APRIL 13, 1992

This nifty dish to Laettner was one of
seven assists for Hurley in the final.

NCAA FINAL FOUR
UNIVERSITY OF MINNESOTA, TWIN CITIES

Celebrating
The Title

JIM WALLACE

A SPECIAL BOND HAS ALWAYS EXISTED BETWEEN THE DUKE
basketball team and its fans – win or lose. The student body is
famous for its outrageous activities during a game in Cameron
Indoor stadium, and their "tent city" often forms weeks in
advance of the next contest. Also unique is the national following the Blue Devils enjoy on the road. No matter if it's California,
New Jersey or Washington, somebody always seems to be
wearing a Duke sweatshirt or baseball cap and can instantly

recite Bobby Hurley's assist total.

That type of devotion made the 1992 national championship even more special. Duke students watched the Final Four games in Cameron while the city of Durham welcomed home the champions with open arms. It was a time for the players and coaches to enjoy the fruits of their hard work and get closer to the people who had cheered them on the whole way.

The Duke contingent also made a second trip to the nation's capital and the White House after an invitation from President George Bush. Finally, the team came together for the final time at the annual awards banquet in Cameron, where it was time to say goodbye to three seniors. In typical Duke fashion, fans stood in line for over an hour outside Cameron to be a part of the curtain call of the 1991-92 season.

JIM WALLACE

The giant screen was set up in Cameron Indoor Stadium for students to watch the Final Four. The Duke pep band kept the festivities lively with "Devil With the Blue Dress On."

The Cameron Crazies were tense and excited as they cheered on the Blue Devils from afar.

Once the victory was sealed, Duke students rushed out to start the traditional victory bonfire. The fire burned into the early hours of the morning as the students danced around the flames.

RON FERRELL

Cameron Indoor Stadium was packed the next day as the team returned from Minneapolis. President H. Keith H. Brodie welcomed the Blue Devils home. Coach K, Christian Laettner, Brian Davis, and Bobby Hurley spoke to the appreciative crowd.

The Durham Chamber of Commerce sponsored a welcome home party for the champions in downtown Durham.

RON FERRELL

The entire Duke team gathered in Washington, D.C., for a visit to the White House.

Coach K presents President George Bush with a Duke championship uniform and basketball.

Coach K and the captains meet the White House press corps on the North Lawn of the White House.

The President invited the women's national champions from Stanford and the Duke team to a free throw shooting contest. Thomas Hill won the prize for the Blue Devils while the President was 1-for-2 from the field, including an impressive reverse layup.

RON FERRELL

The Pentagon invited the Duke team to lunch and a visit of the incredible complex. General Gordon R. Sullivan, Chief of Staff of the U.S. Army (center) was the team's host.

Next stop on the tour was the Arlington National Cemetery. The team stopped at John Kennedy's gravesite and watched the changing of the guard at the Tomb of the Unknown Soldier.

The annual team awards banquet in Cameron Indoor Stadium featured the unveiling of the 1992 national championship banner and a championship video entitled, "A Rhapsody in Blue." The senior class of Ron Burt, Brian Davis and Christian Laettner spoke at the banquet while Thomas Hill and Bobby Hurley were announced as the 1993 team captains.

1991-92 Team Awards

Captains Award
Brian Davis, Christian Laettner

Swett-Baylin Award
(Most Valuable Player)
Christian Laettner, Bobby Hurley

Glenn E. "Ted" Mann Award
(Reserve Contributing Most to Team Morale)
Ron Burt

Dr. Deryl Hart Award
(Top Scholar-Athlete)
Bobby Hurley

Iron Duke Award
(Most Minutes Played)
Bobby Hurley

True Blue Award
(Most Charges Taken)
Brian Davis

Best Field Goal Percentage
Grant Hill

Best Free Throw Percentage
Christian Laettner

Best Rebounding Average
Christian Laettner

Most Assists
Bobby Hurley

Best Defensive Player
Brian Davis

Outstanding Manager
Mark Williams

RON FERRELL

honors

Christian Laettner

National Player of the Year
   (Associated Press/Rupp Award,
   Eastman Award, Naismith Award,
   Wooden Award, U.S. Basketball
   Writers, The Sporting News, Basketball
   Weekly, Basketball Times, Scripps-
   Howard, World Almanac, Joe
   Lapchick Award)

Exemplary Player of the Year
   (Street & Smith's)

Unanimous First Team All-America

ACC Player of the Year

Finalist AAU Sullivan Award

ACC Tournament MVP

First Team All-ACC

All-Final Four

East Regional MVP

First Team All-ACC Tournament

District Player of the Year (USBWA)

First Team All-District (USBWA)

ACC Player of the Week (Jan. 13, Mar. 3)

U.S. Olympic Team

NBA First Round Draft Pick - Minneapolis

LOS ANGELES ATHLETIC CLUB

Laettner's busy
postseason
included trips to
Los Angeles for
the Wooden
Award and an
appearance on
the Arsenio Hall
talk show

MICHAEL LESHNOV / PARAMOUNT PICTURES

Brian Davis

First Team All-ACC Tournament

NBA Second Round Draft Pick - Phoenix

BOB DONNAN

CHRIS BARRY

Bobby Hurley

National Player of the Year Finalist
(Wooden Award and
Eastman Award)

First Team All-America
(NABC, Wooden)

Second Team All-America
(Basketball Times)

Third Team All-America
(AP, UPI, Basketball Weekly)

First Team All-District (USBWA)

Second Team All-ACC

Final Four MVP

All-East Regional

First Team All-ACC Tournament

U.S. Olympic Development Team

Thomas Hill

Third Team All-ACC

ACC Player of the Week (Jan. 20)

BOB DONNAN

Grant Hill

Second Team All-America (UPI)

Honorable Mention All-America (AP)

First Team All-District
(USBWA, Basketball Times)

Second Team All-ACC

All-Final Four

Second Team All-ACC Tournament

U.S. Olympic Development Team

Mike Krzyzewski

National Coach of the Year
(Naismith, The Sporting News)

District Coach of the Year (USBWA)

U.S. Olympic Team Assistant Coach

BOB DONNAN

stats

Record: 34-2 (ACC 14-2, 1st) Home: 13-0 Away: 11-2 Neutral: 10-0

Player	G-GS	Min- Avg	FG-FGA	Pct	3P-3PA	Pct	FT-FTA	Pct	Off-Def	Tot- Avg	PF-FD	AT	TO	BS	ST	Pts - Avg
Laettner, C	35-35	1128-32.2	254- 442	.575	54- 97	.557	189-232	.815	82-193	275- 7.9	90- 1	69	116	32	74	751 -21.5
Hill, T	36-34	1102-30.6	196- 367	.534	37- 91	.407	96-125	.768	44- 77	121- 3.4	75- 1	54	50	16	60	525 -14.6
Hill, G	33-24	1000-30.3	182- 298	.611	0- 1	.000	99-135	.733	49-138	187- 5.7	91- 2	134	80	27	39	463 -14.0
Hurley, B	31-30	1043-33.6	123- 284	.433	59-140	.421	105-133	.789	9- 52	61- 2.0	64- 1	237	109	1	35	410 -13.2
Davis, B	36-35	1111-30.9	140- 291	.481	8- 39	.205	114-154	.740	60-103	163- 4.5	82- 4	69	53	9	42	402 -11.2
Lang, A	34-18	763-22.4	77- 137	.562	0- 0	.000	65- 99	.657	74- 65	139- 4.1	87- 1	23	43	10	20	219 - 6.4
Parks, C	34- 3	435-12.8	60- 105	.571	0- 0	.000	50- 69	.725	30- 51	81- 2.4	57- 0	13	30	35	5	170 - 5.0
Clark, M	34-0	268- 7.9	33- 61	.541	12- 18	.667	21- 27	.778	11- 16	27- 0.8	26- 0	22	21	4	7	99 - 2.9
Meek, E	25- 0	143- 5.7	22- 38	.579	0- 0	.000	18- 36	.500	10- 20	30- 1.2	18- 1	5	6	5	3	62 - 2.5
Blakeney, K	29-1	175- 6.0	13- 23	.565	1- 4	.250	13- 20	.650	5- 19	24- 0.8	10- 0	17	17	0	7	40 - 1.4
Ast, C	14-0	44- 3.1	5- 12	.417	0- 4	.000	6- 9	.667	5- 9	14- 1.0	6- 0	2	4	1	1	16 - 1.1
Burt, R	19-0	38- 2.0	3- 11	.273	0- 0	.000	4- 4	1.000	0- 2	2- 0.1	3- 0	8	4	1	1	10 - 0.5
Team										105						
Duke	36	7250	1108-2069	.536	171-394	.434	780-1043	.748	379-745	1229-34.1	609	653	533	141	294	3167 -88.0
Opponents	36	7250	1033-2213	.467	170-445	.382	379- 583	.650	470-659	1129-31.4	837	557	639	115	232	2615 -72.6

Score by Halves	1	2	OT	Total
Duke:	1558	1586	23	3167
Opponents:	1192	1404	19	2615

Deadball Rebounds
143
107

ATTENDANCE			
SITE	G	TOTAL	AVERAGE
HOME:	13	121,082	9,314
AWAY:	13	168,010	12,924
NEUTRAL:	8	153,733	19,217
TOTAL:	34	442,825	13,024

DUNKS: Duke (146): G. Hill 48, T. Hill 25, Laettner 21, Davis 18, Lang 16, Parks 12, Clark 4, Meek 2
CHARGES TAKEN: Duke (48): Davis 9, Laettner 8, Lang 7, G. Hill 7, T. Hill 6, Hurley 5, Clark 2, Meek 2, Parks 2

Game by Game Statistics (Points-Rebounds-Assists)
*Indicates Starter

Opponent	Result	S	ATT	Clark	Hurley	T. Hill	Lang	Davis	Laettner	G. Hill	Parks
EAST CAROLINA	W 103- 75	H	9,314	17- 5- 4	*20- 0- 7	*16- 1- 0	INJ	* 5- 6- 2	INJ	*15- 6- 3	*16- 8- 1
HARVARD	W 118- 65	H	9,314	10- 4- 1	*13- 1- 4	*17- 1- 4	INJ	*10- 3- 3	*10- 2- 3	*17- 3- 5	15- 6- 0
#St. John's	W 91- 81	N	15,781	1- 0- 1	*14- 2- 8	*14- 2- 2	0- 1- 0	* 7- 3- 2	*26- 7- 1	*15- 3- 1	9- 2- 0
Canisius	W 96- 60	A	16,279	7- 1- 1	* 7- 2- 4	*26- 3- 1	1- 5- 0	* 8- 6- 0	*19- 5- 6	*16-10- 9	INJ
Michigan OT	W 88- 85	A	13,609	2- 0- 0	*26- 2- 7	* 6- 3- 1	2- 1- 0	*12- 7- 0	*24- 8- 1	*16- 6- 0	INJ
WILLIAM & MARY	W 97- 61	H	9,314	3- 1- 2	*13- 3-12	13- 1- 0	7- 3- 0	* 2- 2- 1	*25- 8- 2	*11- 6- 3	*10- 2- 1
Virginia	W 68- 62	A	8,864	2- 0- 1	*11- 1- 8	12- 6- 1	5- 2- 0	* 2- 2- 0	*17- 9- 1	*16- 3- 4	* 3- 4- 0
FLORIDA STATE	W 86- 70	H	9,314	0- 1- 0	* 7- 1- 8	*11- 4- 2	5- 5- 3	*19- 9- 6	*16- 5- 0	*26-10- 1	1- 1- 0
Maryland	W 83- 66	A	14,500	5- 1- 2	* 9- 1- 6	*25- 8- 2	3- 5- 1	* 4- 3- 4	*13- 7- 2	*11- 6- 6	8- 3- 1
GEORGIA TECH	W 97- 84	H	9,314	4- 1- 2	*17- 1-12	*13- 2- 3	0- 2- 2	*14- 9- 1	*33-11- 2	*12- 6- 2	4- 2- 1
N.C. STATE	W 110- 75	H	9,314	6- 2- 2	*19- 6-10	*19- 3- 3	5- 4- 1	* 7- 0- 1	*23- 6- 1	*15- 4- 4	8- 3- 1
UNC CHARLOTTE	W 104- 82	H	9,314	8- 2- 1	* 8- 2-11	*23- 3- 1	11- 5- 0	*10- 5- 1	*24- 6- 1	*12- 1- 1	8- 2- 0
Boston U.	W 95- 85	A	4,108	0- 1- 0	*15- 3- 3	*12- 6- 1	3- 2- 1	*12- 4- 2	*25- 7- 0	*14- 7- 6	8- 3- 0
WAKE FOREST	W 84- 68	H	9,314	2- 1- 0	*12- 4-10	*11- 0- 1	4- 2- 3	*10- 7- 0	*25- 5- 1	*16- 6- 6	4- 1- 0
CLEMSON	W 112- 73	H	9,314	11- 0- 0	*14- 1- 6	*16- 1- 2	12- 7- 0	*11- 0- 3	*11- 5- 2	*10- 5- 4	19- 8- 1
Florida St	W 75- 62	A	13,610	DNP	*11- 1- 7	* 7- 3- 3	8- 4- 0	* 7- 6- 1	*20- 9- 0	*20-10- 2	2- 1- 0
NOTRE DAME	W 100- 71	H	9,314	5- 0- 0	*11- 5- 7	*14- 3- 3	8- 4- 0	*13- 2- 4	*29- 6- 2	*11- 6- 2	5- 4- 0
North Carolina	L 73- 75	A	21,572	0- 1- 0	*11- 0- 6	*16- 5- 0	3- 4- 0	*17- 5- 0	*12-12- 1	*10- 3- 7	4- 0- 0
Louisiana St	W 77- 67	A	13,846	0- 0- 0	INJ	*15- 5- 4	*12- 5- 3	* 8- 2- 1	*22-10- 3	*16- 9- 6	4- 4- 2
Georgia Tech	W 71- 62	A	10,026	0- 0- 0	INJ	*18- 3- 0	* 5- 1- 0	*11- 5- 3	*15- 8- 5	*20- 6- 5	2- 1- 1
N.C. State	W 71- 63	A	12,400	5- 0- 0	INJ	*16- 3- 3	* 6- 2- 1	* 8- 4- 5	*16- 6- 2	*20- 6- 6	0- 2- 0
MARYLAND	W 91- 89	H	9,314	0- 0- 0	INJ	*13- 4- 2	*12- 6- 0	*19- 4- 4	*30- 8- 2	*14- 4- 6	3- 1- 1
Wake Forest	L 68- 72	A	14,673	0- 1- 1	INJ	*20- 1- 1	* 6- 6- 0	*12- 1- 1	*18- 4- 2	*12- 6- 5	0- 0- 0
VIRGINIA	W 76- 67	H	9,314	0- 0- 0	4- 2- 9	*11- 4- 3	* 7- 5- 1	*10- 6- 2	*32-13- 1	INJ	6- 2- 0
UCLA	W 75- 65	A	13,023	0- 0- 0	*11- 0- 4	* 8- 2- 1	* 5- 9- 1	*19-11- 4	*29-13- 2	INJ	0- 1- 0
Clemson	W 98- 97	A	11,500	0- 0- 3	*11- 2- 8	*11- 6- 0	*14- 7- 1	*30- 6- 2	*23- 9- 5	INJ	2- 4- 0
NORTH CAROLINA	W 89- 77	H	9,314	DNP	*19- 2- 9	*18- 4- 1	*10- 5- 1	* 8- 5- 4	*26- 8- 3	8- 4- 3	0- 0- 0
!Maryland	W 94- 87	N	23,532	0- 0- 0	*16- 2-13	*12- 3- 1	* 8- 1- 2	*17- 6- 1	*33-16- 3	5- 4- 0	3- 5- 0
!Georgia Tech	W 89- 76	N	23,532	2- 1- 0	*17- 1- 2	*10- 1- 2	* 9- 4- 0	*17- 6- 1	*15- 5- 5	13- 5- 5	4- 1- 3
!North Carolina	W 94- 74	N	23,532	0- 0- 0	*11- 2-11	*13- 3- 0	*11- 4- 1	*12- 2- 4	*25-10- 0	20- 3- 7	0- 0- 0
^Campbell	W 82- 56	N	15,800	4- 2- 0	*10- 3-10	*20- 5- 1	* 6- 3- 1	* 7- 2- 3	*22- 9- 4	5- 5- 5	4- 5- 0
^Iowa	W 75- 62	N	15,800	0- 1- 0	*12- 4- 9	*10- 5- 2	* 2- 8- 0	*21-10- 0	*19- 8- 1	11- 4- 0	0- 0- 0
•Seton Hall	W 81- 69	N	17,878	0- 0- 1	* 4- 1- 7	*13- 5- 1	*16- 7- 0	*15- 4- 2	*16- 6- 1	13- 4- 2	2- 1- 0
•Kentucky OT	W 104-103	N	17,878	0- 0- 0	*22- 3-10	*19- 3- 2	* 4- 3- 0	*13- 5- 1	*31- 7- 3	11-10- 7	4- 0- 0
$Indiana	W 81- 78	N	50,379	5- 1- 0	*26- 0- 4	*11- 2- 0	* 4- 3- 0	* 5- 5- 0	* 8-10- 1	14- 6- 6	8- 1- 0
$Michigan	W 71- 51	N	50,379	0- 0- 0	* 9- 3- 7	*16- 7- 0	* 5- 4- 0	0- 0- 0	*19- 7- 0	*18-10- 5	4- 3- 0

#ACC/BIG EAST CHALLENGE @ Greensboro, N.C
!ACC Tournament, Charlotte, N.C. (First-Place)
^NCAA First and Second Rounds, Greensboro, N.C.
•NCAA East Regional, Philadelphia, Pa.
$NCAA Final Four, Minneapolis, Minn.

Back To Back

By Bill Brill

BRIAN SPURLOCK

BACK TO BACK.

It has a nice ring to it.

It works well with T-shirts.

It's driving opponents crazy.

And, as we shall see, it is an astonishing performance.

Les Robinson, the North Carolina State coach, had this evaluation of Duke's consecutive NCAA

championships. "It will be at least four or five years before we truly appreciate what Duke has done," he said. "It is truly amazing."

There are those basketball experts who believe there won't be another back-to-back in our lifetime. They do not include Duke fans, of course, who serenaded their champions in the closing seconds at Minneapolis with a "Three-peat" cheer.

What is essential to understand about the two national titles is that to properly evaluate just what the men of Krzyzewski have achieved, it is required to examine the seven-year period, dating back to 1986, during which the Blue Devils reached the Final Four every year except 1987.

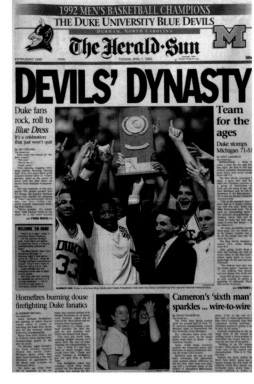

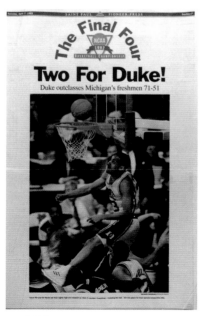

Just as winning for the first time in 1991, unexpected as it was, somehow legitimized the Final Four string, winning again in 1992 elevated Duke to new levels, above and beyond opposition.

The "D" word was fashionable again for the first time since John Wooden and UCLA adopted the NCAA Tournament as their own invitational for a dozen years, ending in 1975.

If Duke doesn't stand for dynasty, at least it starts with the same letter. "The Dukes of Destiny" was the way CBS broadcaster Jim Nantz described it as the Michigan game ended in the Metrodome.

Before discussing the merits of what the Blue Devils have done, it is required to examine some numbers. You can make too much of statistics in some cases, but for Duke basketball, it is the evidence of glory.

To wit:

Duke is the first team to win consecutive NCAA titles in 19 years.

Only five other schools have achieved that feat, only one in modern history. Oklahoma State won in 1945 and 1946 when the school was known as Oklahoma A&M and its center was 7-footer Bob Kurland. Kentucky followed with titles in 1948 and 1949, and center Alex Groza was the dominant performer. San Francisco swept two in a row in 1955 and 1956 with Bill Russell playing the pivot. Cincinnati won in 1961 and again in 1962.

Then came the Wooden years: 1964, beating Duke in the championship game, and 1965. Then starting in 1967, a remarkable seven crowns in a row, five of them with centers Lew Alcindor and Bill Walton.

A pattern is established here. While it's nice to have good players at every position, winning two in a row (or more) required a great big man. Hello, Christian Laettner.

All of the repeat winners played in the era before multiple teams from conference were permitted in the NCAA Tournament.

Oklahoma A&M and Kentucky, the first double winners, played when there were just eight teams in the field. They only needed to win three games for the championship. There was no such thing as the Final Four.

By 1955, the field had expanded to 24 schools and San Francisco became the first titlist to play five games. The next season, the Dons got an opening round bye and required just two victories to reach the semifinals.

Every one of UCLA's champions except the last one, in 1975, played when only the conference champions and independents made the field. The Bruins always had an opening bye. They needed two wins to get to the Final Four. Only in Wooden's last season did UCLA have to win five games for the championship.

Duke started its run to immortality and a place in history in 1986, the year after the field expanded to the present format of 64 teams, with no byes. Even more critical, the regional brackets had now been balanced by moving teams around, and no longer did East play Southeast and Midwest meet West in the opening semifinals. The pairings were rotated. UCLA always met the champion of the Midwest in the semifinal game until it was beaten by N.C. State in 1974 in Greensboro.

The 64-team field, meticulously balanced by the NCAA Basketball Committee of nine, assures the most difficult possible path to the championship. If

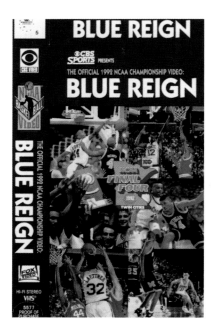

there is a weak region - the West was notoriously soft in UCLA's banner days - the committee simply moves strong teams from around the country to even things out.

Everybody concedes that winning the NCAAs today is far more difficult than it was prior to multiple conference entries, beginning in 1975. Yet Duke's present run began after expansion.

Let's go back to 1975, when the field was increased to 32 teams. Since then, only five schools have made the Final Four in successive years. Houston did it three times in a row with Hakeem Olajuwan (1982-84), without ever winning a championship. North Carolina (1981-82), Louisville (1982-83), Georgetown (1984-85), and UNLV (1990-91) were the others.

Of that group, Georgetown was the only team to reach the title game the year after winning the championship. The Hoyas were upset by Villanova in 1985 in Lexington, Ky.

North Carolina got to the finals in 1981, losing to Indiana, before beating Georgetown the following season for Dean Smith's lone NCAA crown. Louisville was beaten in the semifinals in both seasons.

Contrast that with Duke, which has now been to the Final Four five times in a row and six of the past seven. Other than UCLA's skein of seven straight, the only other school to appear in five straight Final Fours was Cincinnati, 1959-63.

Duke has played in three straight championship games, having lost to UNLV in 1990. Besides UCLA's record seven straight title appearances, the only other school ever to play three consecutive times in the finals were Ohio State (1960-62) and Cincinnati (1961-63).

There are other ways of evaluating just how significant Duke's recent achievements have been.

Since the field expanded to 64 teams, Mike Krzyzewski's NCAA record is 33-6. The only coaches in history who have won more games than that are Smith, the leader with 49; Wooden (47-10) and Bob Knight (35-13). Denny Crum is 33-16. For all his four championships, Adolph Rupp's overall NCAA record was 30-18. Jerry Tarkanian finished his college career at 31-13.

Even more impressive:

During the four-year careers of Laettner and Brian Davis, Duke posted a 21-2 NCAA record. (Bobby Hurley will take a 17-1 record into his senior season).

In that same span, only two *conferences*, the Big Ten and Big East, have won more NCAA games than the Blue Devils. The Big East has won 18 games, the Pacific-10 has 14 wins, and the Southeastern Conference 11. Along with the ACC, those are considered to be the Big Six of college hoops.

That statistic is important enough to review twice. Collectively, only two entire leagues have won more NCAA games

than the Blue Devils since 1989.

Since the 64-team field was adopted in 1985, Duke has been to the Final Four six times. Kansas and UNLV have been there three times; Indiana and Michigan have made it twice. Nobody else has gone more than once.

Also, Duke has played in four championship games; of all the others, only Michigan and Kansas have gotten to the finals twice. The NCAA's balancing act, scholarship limits and television money have created a legitimate parity throughout the country. Only Duke appears unaffected.

Since the Blue Devils began their run in 1986, no other *league* has produced as many Final Four entries. While Duke has been going year after year, the Big Ten has advanced five teams, the Big Eight four, the Big East three.

What is more intriguing is that Duke has gotten to the Final Four in a variety of ways. It was the number one seed in 1986 when the Blue Devils finished 37-3, a national record for wins that, in this era of reduced schedules, likely will never be broken.

The 1992 team also led the nation in victories with 34 in a season when only one other school won as many as 30. Duke also was the first team since North Carolina in 1982 to start the year No. 1, finish it the same way, and also win the NCAA. Unbeaten Indiana in 1976 was the last team to be rated number one every week, as were the Blue Devils in 1992.

In between the two top-rated teams, Duke produced four Final Four teams that were not favored to make it out of the regional. And rarely did anybody do the Devils any favors. Three consecutive seasons, 1988-90, Duke won the NCAA East Regional as the number two seed, in each occasion beating the number one seed in the championship game. Temple, Georgetown and Connecticut all fell, the latter on the first of Laettner's buzzer-beating miracle shots.

In Duke's first championship season, the Blue Devils came out of the Midwest for the lone time, again as the number two seed.

CHUCK LIDDY

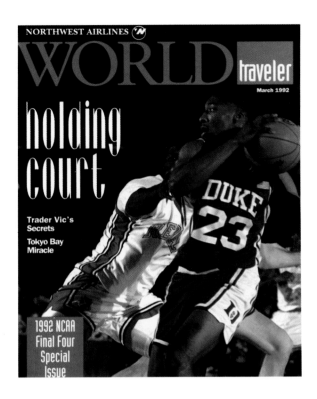

NORTHWEST AIRLINES

WORLD traveler

March 1992

holding court

Trader Vic's
Secrets

Tokyo Bay
Miracle

1992 NCAA
Final Four
Special
Issue

The back-to-back titles were achieved in a totally different manner by totally different teams, even though most of the personnel was the same.

Lost in the frenzy created by the upset of UNLV in 1991 was the realization that Duke dominated the tournament throughout. Yet this was a team which lost six regular season games, including blowouts at Virginia and Wake Forest, then was crushed by 22 points by North Carolina in the ACC Tournament final.

But Coach K got his troops back on track in a hurry. Duke had only one close game during the 1991 NCAA Tournament, against a veteran UNLV team that had beaten the Blue Devils by 30 points the previous national championship game.

Duke shot better than 50 percent in every NCAA game, the only team to do that against UNLV all season. Midwest Regional games against Iowa, Connecticut and St. John's were settled by halftime. The closest game was 14 points.

Even the title contest against Kansas wasn't memorable. Duke led the entire game and was ahead by 14 points with three minutes left, making the final score of 72-65 somewhat deceiving.

This season, the Blue Devils breezed past Campbell and Iowa (again), and produced a workmanlike effort against Seton Hall in a battle of old friends (Coach K and P.J. Carlesimo) and brothers (Bobby and Danny Hurley).

The East title game against Kentucky already has been immortalized by "The Shot," Laettner's spinning 17-footer after the three-quarter-court pass from Grant Hill that gave Duke the 104-103 overtime victory. It was a far narrower escape than against UNLV the previous year.

"It was one of the best games I've ever seen," said Carlesimo, who served with Coach K as an assistant on the 1992 U.S. Olympic team.

"Most likely it was the best tournament game ever," said Al McGuire.

"Every single play it seemed like they would rise to the occasion," said Kansas coach Roy Williams, "and make one great play after another."

In the Final Four, in a departure from the past, Duke played poor offense and trailed at the half of each game. But Indiana was shut down starting the second half with some stunning defense, after which the Blue Devils held Michigan to just 20 points in the last period of the championship game.

Interestingly, each championship sea-

son is destined to be known more for games that occurred before the finals - against UNLV in 1991 and Kentucky in 1992. The NCAA even got caught in that trap. A video produced for a pre-Final Four banquet in Minneapolis ostensibly focused on previous national championship games. But when it got to 1991, highlights of the Duke-UNLV game were shown. "I thought we played for the championship," said Kansas' Williams.

Duke has made its march to college basketball's pinnacle every way possible. The only given has been Coach K. Duke has won when it was healthy and when it played through injuries, as it did in 1992 when Hurley missed five games with a broken foot and Grant Hill was sidelined awhile with a sprained ankle. Brian Davis played just briefly against Michigan because of a damaged ankle. The Blue Devils were unbeaten when they were well.

Duke has won when it was favored, and when it was an underdog. It has won games with ease and with last-second shots. Nobody ever said building a winner came easily, or without some good fortune.

Through it all has been the standards established by Krzyzewski. Every season, rugged non-conference games have been scheduled in February to prepare the team for March Madness. The better to see first hand what the perils may be.

Surely it has worked. Krzyzewski has proved himself as a March coach - three ACC Tournament titles, six regional championships.

Best of all, however, has been April. For that is when Back-to-Back took place.

Krzyzewski's peers appreciate the achievement.

"I like the way Coach K went at it," said McGuire, who won the NCAA in 1977 in his final game with Marquette, "when he said 'We're not defending a championship, we're pursuing it.'"

"I think it's going to take time to put it into perspective," said Carlesimo, whose team lost in the finals to Michigan in 1989 after beating Duke in the NCAA semifinals. "But it's absolutely amazing what Duke has done."

Williams, the former North Carolina assistant coach, said, "Six of seven years (in the Final Four), and two national championships in a row. I think Mike ought to go up on top of the mountain and stay there the rest of his life and let the rest of us have a chance at some things."

But there's also the future to ponder. Speaking at Cameron Indoor Stadium after the triumphant return from Minneapolis, Coach K said with a grin, "Last year, I said I wondered where a second (banner) would hang. Now we've got to do it.

"I'm probably stupid for saying this, but I wonder where a third one might go?"

CHUCK LIDDY

BOB DONNAN

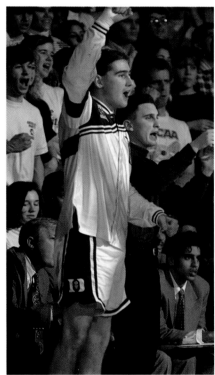
BOB DONNAN

CHUCK LIDDY

After celebrating the school's first national basketball championship in 1991, Duke had to overcome a tough schedule and numerous injuries (including a broken foot to point guard Bobby Hurley) to repeat the accomplishment in 1992, sparking talk of a Blue Devil dynasty among the team's fans.

one last look...

KEVIN KEISTER

BRIAN SPURLOCK

BOB DONNAN

CHUCK LIDDY

SEAN OSER

BOB DONNAN

BOB DONNAN

BOB DONNAN

SEAN OSER

113